Heart Felt

Heart Felt

THE JENNA COOPER STORY

John Mabry

ISBN-13: 9780692717592
ISBN-10: 0692717595
Library of Congress Control Number: 2016912224
InspireU Publishing, Lincoln, NE
Second Edition

Jenna Marie Cooper
September 28, 1982 – April 25, 2004

*"I hope one day I can be an inspiration to someone
else to follow your dreams and be who you truly are inside."*

To Ellen, William and Billy
Thank you for allowing me to share Jenna's story. I do believe you had it right
when you called her a miracle. And thank you for your patience, your hospitality
and your Kentucky kindness, from the bottom of my heart.

To Emma, Alex and Jack
Thank you for enduring the challenges of having me for a father. No easy
assignment, for sure. The combination of love and pride I have for you is
immeasurable.

To Anna
Thank you for your love, encouragement and support. I am not sure I would
have finished this without your heart-felt kicks in the caboose. I love you. Can't
wait to show you Prospect, Kentucky. It is beautiful there.

Prologue

Twelve years later, I still remember the phone call well. It was about 9 a.m. on a Sunday morning, April 25, 2004. I took the call in the kitchen.

Peter Salter, city editor for the Lincoln Journal Star, called to let me know that a University of Nebraska soccer player had been shot at a party early that morning.

Peter called me because I was the Journal Star's sports editor at the time, and I also covered the Nebraska women's soccer team. He did not have a lot of the details yet, but he said he thought it was the captain of the team. He did not know how badly they had been hurt. He just thought I should know that something bad and newsworthy had happened on the local sports scene.

I had a feeling I knew who it was, and I all I could think about was how in the world something like that could have happened.

I called the team's coach, John Walker, and asked if he could share anything with me. He was serious and somber, but he politely told me what he knew or at least what he felt comfortable sharing at the time.

There had been a shooting at a party. Somehow, the one bullet that had been fired hit two people.

One of them was Jenna.

Introduction

*Every player who comes to Nebraska will
know the story of Jenna Cooper.*

John Walker

Jenna Cooper's story started, for me, on a bright August day in 2001.
That's when I talked to her for the first time, just as she was starting her collegiate soccer career. She was a freshman at the University of Nebraska, a college
star in the making, although the making in her case didn't take long.

I needed a preseason feature on the Cornhuskers, so I headed to the Abbott
Sports Complex in northeast Lincoln to see the speedy, left-footed rookie
from Kentucky. She was happy to talk and answer my questions, but she also
seemed to think it was strange that I wanted to talk to her – a freshman.

She was more interested in showing off her ride – a red Jeep Wrangler.
The roll bar said 'Cooper.' There was a big, white No. 3 on the side. I didn't
know it at the time, but that Jeep was every bit Jenna. "I take this off-road a
lot," she told me. "This is my hobby off the soccer field."

On road or off, those wheels could go around or through obstacles,
depending on the circumstances. That is how Jenna played soccer, even
though she was often one of the smallest players on the field. She was not
afraid to go around or through, and she could do both with ease. Her style

of play was fearless – "electric" according to her coach – and her left foot was vicious when it met a soccer ball full-on.

She told me that day why she wore No. 3 – a tribute to late race-car legend Dale Earnhardt – and she explained why she chose to come to Nebraska when she could have played just about anywhere in the nation.

"Strictly the way they play, with the high-pressure," she said. "It's kind of an extreme way to play."

Jenna had an extreme spirit. Coaches said her play was electric. So was her smile. She came to Nebraska a little wide-eyed and nervous. She was also homesick at first, but as she started getting to know her teammates, she felt as home as could be. She was confident without being cocky. More humble than not. She wondered why I would want to talk to her, just being a freshman and all. But when I went looking for story ideas, Jenna seemed like a natural.

I wrote about how fast she was, what a standout defender she was and how she was unfazed in her first college game – a 1-0 victory over mighty North Carolina. And it was Jenna who scored the game's only goal in a smashing debut. I just didn't write about her heart, but we will get to that, because what I came to know is that it's a heart like no other.

I have learned a lot about Jenna since that summer day when I met her, like how she fell in love with soccer in the rain and how she struggled with focus problems in school and how she had to organize her food on the plate just so before she could eat and how fortunate she felt in life, even in tough times.

I learned that her favorite place on earth was an isolated area in the Kentucky woods just east of Louisville, in Prospect. It's where the Wolf Pen Branch Mill churned out flour in the late 19th century, and it's where Jenna loved to take her cocker spaniel, Lady, for a run and her Jeep for a drive.

Even in the cold and gray of winter, it is spectacular there. It's a peaceful spot, until you get close to the water rushing past, or until a flock of geese makes a surprise pass overhead. The walking trail through the forest was once the road to Cincinnati. Now it's a narrow highway of dirt, moss and leaves just south of the Ohio River and the Kentucky-Indiana border. As a girl, Jenna was taken with the land where her father, William, was raised with his brother and sister. In the words of Jenna's brother, Billy, it's "never not pretty."

Several members of William's family are buried there, including his parents. After Jenna's grandfather 'Poppy' died, she wrote an essay for school that included some of her thoughts about that sanctuary where pain had no place. She was 16.

The woods that surrounded the cemetery were lavish. It seemed that no matter what was troubling you, when you walked down that dirt road and through the woods and cemetery, all troubles ceased to exist.

CHAPTER 1

A Gut-Wrenching Time

THERE IS SOMETHING NOT QUITE right about a woman born on Valentine's Day ending up with a broken heart.

When Wendy Davies celebrated her 39th birthday on Feb. 14, 2004, she seemed to be in excellent health. Life in Luxembourg, Wis., was rolling along for Wendy and her husband, Garth, and their two young children – Luke and Emily. It was time to focus on raising a family, with the normal bumps and bruises that come attached to that adventure.

But the Davies were not prepared for the challenge that ambushed them that winter. Wendy's health took a bad turn in a hurry, and by late February, the outlook was not good at all. Wendy's heart was failing. She was fighting for her life, and the family was struggling to figure out what had hit them.

The trouble started just a few days after the family celebrated Emily's first birthday, on Feb. 23. Wendy never had a health issue of any significance, and there was no history of heart trouble in her family. But her condition declined quickly.

Doctors struggled at first to identify the exact cause of the problem, but there was no question that this was a life-threatening situation. Wendy was airlifted to the medical center at the University of Wisconsin in Madison on Feb. 28. A biopsy showed that she had giant cell myocarditis, a condition that leads to severe inflammation, so much so that it overpowers the heart muscle cells.

"Within two days of when she arrived here, she was getting worse," said cardiologist Maryl Johnson, "and in fact, so bad, that they ended up putting heart pumps in to support the right and left side of her heart to keep her alive."

A bi-ventricular assist device was installed to allow Wendy's heart to continue to pump blood to the rest of the body. While doctors worked to keep his wife alive, Garth was trying to prepare for another birthday. Luke Davies turned 4 on March 2, the day things looked the darkest for his mom. The surgery was rough. Her heart was too weak to sustain her much longer.

Every day seemed to be worse than the last, and Garth couldn't help but think that he was not far from being a widower with two toddlers. He prayed.

Please, God, let her make it another day.

The thought of losing his wife was horrible enough, but the thought of Luke's birthday coming every year attached to the memory of his mother's death was unbearable.

After a long struggle that night, Wendy pulled through. The machine that became part of her was working. But Wendy was far from being out of the woods. She spent the next week in a coma. And Garth kept praying. He wasn't sure things were that much better. Wendy was in the hospital until April 18, when she went home to wait and hope for a transplant heart. Two days later, she had a stroke. Her mom and Garth rushed her back to Madison. More waiting. More praying.

"I thought she was going to die," Garth said.

The only hope was a new heart.

Early in the morning of April 26 – around 3 a.m. – Wendy called the nurse's station to ask for some juice. It seemed like a simple request, but she was told it wasn't a good time for refreshments. The nurse at UW Hospital said Wendy had to keep her system clean because of the potential for major surgery later in the day.

"We think we might have a heart for you."

That news came to Wisconsin as an impromptu soccer game was going on, at the oddest of hours, under the lights in Lincoln. The fact that a good heart might be on its way was incredible news for the Davies family, but it was tempered with curious thoughts of how the heart became available. Garth couldn't help but wonder.

"It was a gut-wrenching time because we knew someone had to die for that to take place."

CHAPTER 2

The Formula of Jenna

I will wear a dress, and sometimes it will be pink. I spend time
doing my hair and makeup, and then I will put on perfume.
I will talk cute with a little charm, but do not let these things
fool you. I am a tom-boy at heart. The things that cannot be
seen on the surface are the things that mean the most to me.
I play soccer, work in the garage, and drive race cars.
I am just a girl from Kentucky…

JENNA COOPER (WRITTEN AS PART OF A COLLEGE
ASSIGNMENT, JANUARY 15, 2004)

THAT GIRL WAS A KICKER from the very start.

Her mom could feel it. Her dad could see it.

That Cooper baby moved from one side to another, giving the womb regular workouts, sometimes putting on an aerobic show for Ellen's co-workers at Bacon's Department Store in Louisville. Everyone marveled at the prenatal mobility of Ellen and William's second child.

The Coopers already had a son, Billy, who was 2. They did not know if their second would be a boy or a girl, but Ellen had a feeling. It was no secret she was hoping for a girl. She also wished for a smoother delivery the second time around. It took 26 hours to deliver Billy, and when he arrived on Jan. 8, 1980, he wasn't breathing. He was blue.

"It scared us to death," William said. But after a day in intensive care, Billy pulled through. A gift from the heavens. A girl needs her big brother.

The second childbirth was everything Ellen wanted – a baby girl and a trouble-free delivery. Jenna Marie Cooper breezed into the world on September 28, 1982. After Billy, five hours of labor didn't seem like quite the same struggle, and Jenna couldn't have been healthier when she checked in at 7 pounds, 7 ounces. Ellen, a buyer for Bacon's, chose 'Jenna' after talking to a work associate in California who had that name. It was not a common name at the time, and that added to its appeal. Ellen chose Marie as the middle name because she thought it was a good Christian name.

Some family members were not totally sold on the title of Jenna Marie, but it grew on them. Just as the thought of having a girl grew on William. He wondered if a daughter would be as excited about the things he was excited about – race cars and motorcycles. His passion and his livelihood. William and his brother ran a motorcycle shop in Louisville. It didn't take long for Jenna to show her father he might have gotten more than he bargained for. "She was a rough little thing," William said.

A rough little thing who didn't fuss much at all as a baby. She rarely cried. She made parenting easy from the start. As an infant, she did not want to be rocked to sleep. Put her in bed and be done with it. No commotion.

As a toddler, Jenna had a gift for making the best of a bad situation. One of Jenna's uncles – Ellen's brother, Doug – was paralyzed from the chest down when he was 17, the result of a cliff-climbing accident. At age 3, Jenna would climb aboard Uncle Doug's wheelchair and ride with him as his pint-size physical and spiritual therapist.

With Dad, ready to roll

She would say: "Uncle Doug, I can show you how to walk. Just put one foot here and the next foot here...."

Around that time, Ellen and William were divorced, after 16 years of marriage. They tried to keep the split as smooth as possible for the sake of their two kids. Billy had to be the big kid and try to explain things, after Ellen and William sat the kids down on the couch and told them what was happening. Even in difficult times, Jenna always felt like she was the luckiest person on earth. She was sad her parents were not going to be living together but happy she would have two places to call home.

What troubled Jenna and Billy most was the fear they would not get to see their father. Jenna was a daddy's girl, and it would have been devastating to be away from her dad. But the kids spent weekends with William and quite a few weeks during the year when Ellen was on the road, so Dad was still a big part of their lives.

When she was barely school age, about 5 or 6, Jenna noticed that the backyard of her father's home in Louisville needed some sprucing up. The neighbor behind William Cooper's place had a garden full of bright colors. Dad's place didn't stack up in Jenna's eyes, so she went to the garage looking for a quick fix.

Spray paint.

Jenna grabbed all the cans she could find – blue, gold, bright green – and went to work. The heck with seeding and watering and waiting. Even with both hands, she could barely make the nozzles on the spray cans function. But in a few minutes, Dad's yard was as bright as the showplace on the other side of the fence.

"It actually looked kind of cool for a while, a couple of days," William said.

Jenna's early competitive fun was highlighted by bike races with her brother. The racing seed was planted by William, who grew up with a passion for motorcycles and speed. Jenna and Billy raced on a course they created in their dad's backyard. Jenna, always looking for an edge, cut an opening in a little holly bush. The gap allowed her to cruise to victory unhindered while her brother had to do everything in his power to avoid a face full of prickly foliage.

Like most kids at pre-school age, Jenna gave soccer a try early. She didn't show a lot of interest in the game – or during a game. In those rare instances when she was asked to play goalkeeper, Jenna would spend much of the time running around the back of the goal to give Dad kisses and hugs. Coaches would tell the Coopers that it was a good thing their daughter was so cute because her soccer skills were not that pretty.

Billy and Jenna and their bikes. Numbers 15 and 3, the way it had to be.

But then on a rainy day in Louisville, Jenna fell in love with the sport. She was 7. The rain was heavy, but she was running around without a care in the mud and puddles that had collected in her dad's front yard. She was wearing William's raincoat, doing face-plants in the water and kicking the ball all over the place, having the time of her life on what otherwise seemed like a miserable day.

"I had never seen her laugh so much in her life," William said.

That day, the game took on a different meaning for her. It was a game that allowed her to run wild and cut loose, to get dirty. That was the day she decided she wanted to be a soccer player.

There was definitely athletic blood in the family, though soccer was never part of the picture. Ellen was the third of Pat and Arthur McLaughlin's eight kids. In high school, she played softball, field hockey, tennis and basketball. She was a star at Assumption in Louisville. It was before women's basketball was recognized as an official NCAA sport – Title IX legislation had not come into play. But the Cardinals made it to the national women's tournament while Ellen was on the team, as a forward and key contributor.

The major universities in Lexington and Louisville boast two of the most tradition-rich basketball programs in the nation. Ellen joked "they had to come up with a new sport" to get Billy and Jenna interested. While soccer had been around for decades in other parts of the world, it was not a well-known activity in the Bluegrass State. There was almost no interest in soccer in Kentucky when Ellen was growing up. But it had gained in popularity when Billy and Jenna were kids.

Soccer was another way for Jenna and Billy to bond. They were always close but when their parents split in 1985, Jenna and Billy became closer. Billy was Jenna's first soccer coach, if only in an unofficial capacity. Jenna's soccer career started with one-on-one showdowns with Billy in the backyard of their mom's home in Louisville. Playing with Billy and his friends toughened Jenna.

Most young soccer players with a goal at home have a mini net. The Coopers had the real deal. William and Billy built the goal in Ellen's back-yard so the height and width were about a foot smaller than regulation, just to make sure the Cooper kids were just that much more precise in their scoring attempts. It wasn't long before Jenna was excelling on the soccer field, even though she was one of the smaller players.

That success was born of speed and toughness and the desire to be active all the time. No TV. Jenna would much rather have all the kids out in the backyard playing. No sitting around. She would order friends and cousins to get off their butts and get outside.

And when Jenna moved, she could really move. Her dad called her "Jitterbug" because her feet were so quick. She could fly. The other kids in her middle school knew the drill. On field day, the boys would be all fired up to show off their flash until they found out Jenna had signed up for the sprints. Take it easy on the other kids in gym class, her PE teacher would ask.

She was almost always upbeat and full of energy as a kid, but when her dog, Lady, was hit by a car and killed, Jenna was devastated. The driver did not stop after hitting Lady, and Jenna could not understand that. How could someone do that, take a life, and just move on? It was not something she got over quickly.

Jenna attended high school at an all-girl Catholic School in Louisville. In no time, she was a star in the Sacred Heart soccer program, a player with few peers, blessed with a combination of speed and talent and a mighty left foot. She became a leader in the soccer program but was never chosen as team captain, a point of some frustration. But she would tell Ellen often that she was just happy "to have my cleats on the field."

Jenna was a good student despite significant hurdles. Midway through high school, Jenna expressed some concerns about her inability to stay focused in class. She was diagnosed with dyslexia and attention deficit disorder and began taking medication for the problem. Her dad said she joked about how she ended up with the condition. "She said, 'I know Mom doesn't have ADD, so I'm sure you do, Dad,' so she was kind of blaming that on me." Focus was often a problem for her, but she put in the extra time to study when things were not clear. As with most teenage students, some things captured her attention more than others. Math was the subject that grabbed her.

She was a popular student and would look out for those who were not. At lunch time, she would often find a new student or someone sitting alone, and she would join them to keep them company. She was active in various clubs and teachers would talk about what a treat it was to have Jenna in their classes, except for a minor problem with the dress code. Jenna wasn't big on the required uniform and would often be asked to go home and get the clothes she was supposed to be wearing as part of the program at Sacred Heart.

When a representative from the Kentucky Organ Donor Affiliates organization came to talk to Sacred Heart students about organ donation, Jenna was all ears. She didn't make a big production of it, but she told friends she was going to sign the back of her driver's license to confirm her commitment to being a donor. She had no doubt it was the right thing to do.

That driver's license was like gold for Jenna. She grew up driving motorbikes and ATV's around the Cooper farm and anywhere she could get out and ride. Getting her license was a big, big deal. And around the time of her 16th birthday, she became the proud owner of a 1989 red Jeep Wrangler.

She and her dad spent a good part of 1989 with that Jeep. William, aka Rebel, put in a custom seat and roll cage. It was a special time for him as he reflected on having a Jeep of his own – a 1948 model that had to take the place of a horse. He couldn't have the four-legged ride because of allergies, so his parents helped him get a Jeep.

Jenna put in a lot of hours getting her Wrangler road and off-road ready. She worked in a doctor's office to save money for accessories – about $1,200 worth. She loved that Jeep. It became part of her. Outside of soccer, Jenna's passion was in the garage. It was another form of the thrill of the chase, and it would come while helping her dad and brother in their racing hobby. They were in William's garage all the time, working on motorcycles and cars and Jenna's Jeep. She loved it – the mechanic work, the driving, the tires, the grease – all of it.

She had a motor for racing, and as a senior at Sacred Heart, Jenna turned in the following English paper on Sept. 28, 2000, her 18th birthday:

Formula 1: The Formula of Me

Ratchets click. Power tools scream. Each crew prepares the means for one to step up to another level of competition. The smell of specially formulated gasoline fills the air. The odor is crisp and refreshing reminding me of the way the air fills my lungs and nostrils when I step outside on a cold day.

A roaring V-12 engine makes the car a power house. Endurance and responsiveness to environment protect the jaguar from the predators of nature; the Formula 1, too, possesses these characteristics for survival. Nothing is done in moderation; every tool and mechanical component that works on or is part of the car performs at an extreme level. It accelerates fast, brakes quickly, crashes hard, and wins big. Performance, endurance, and strength are vital to survival accompanied by success.

Advancement of technology is a reminder that there are no limits. When one works with machine unnatural things can be done, and higher levels of competition can be reached. There is always room for improvement. Happiness and enjoyment are found in the creativity and genius involved with enhancing performance of the car, not in satisfaction for what has already been developed. I love working on cars and find my drive and motivation comes from never allowing myself to settle for second best.

The Formula 1 race car best compares to my personality and much of what I believe in life. The characteristics of the machine and the drive and motivation in the work to surpass existing limits relate to me directly. I never stop to gaze at the present because I feel that time should not be wasted on concern for what is already here; time should be spent finding ways to improve the old and enhance the best.

There is excitement in being fearless, living on the edge and doing something no one else has ever done. There is never time to waste because my life is filled with goals to accomplish and barriers to break. I "drop the hammer" along the straightaways by taking care of simple tasks with speed and efficiency, and I slow down for the turns by paying attention to detail and technique. Living the life of a race car driver gives me a sense of control in a world that is realistically uncontrollable.

Jenna with her parents on Sacred Heart Senior Day

CHAPTER 3

Kentucky Cornhusker

*When it came time for college, I found out that I had a lot more to
learn about the world that I could not have possibly learned living
with my family in the same city I have lived in all my life. I needed
to find independence and the true me. I moved away from home
to play soccer and attend school at the University of Nebraska.*

JENNA'S SOCCER SKILLS WERE NO secret to women's college programs across
the country. The Coopers received more than 100 recruiting letters, from
schools coast to coast.

In the spring of 2000, Jenna played in the Blue Chip Invitational in
Cincinnati, a showcase event attended by college coaches looking for elite
talent. While Jenna might have been considered smallish in stature, she made
a big impression at the tournament. She was quickly identified as a top-tier
recruit.

The letters from college coaches came in bunches.

Kentucky: "I want to be honest with you from the start of this recruiting
process. We want you to come to UK! I know you could make an impact right
away!"

Ohio State: "You did a nice job getting up and down the flanks, but I thought
when you moved up front, you took things over. Keep up the good work!"

Purdue: "You possess both pace and a thunderous left foot – both of
which will serve you well as you make the transition to the college game. I

thought the way you threw yourself into tackles and your toughness separated you from most every other player on the pitch."

Tennessee: "I was impressed with your dynamic play and toughness."

Marquette (big letters EN Fuego!): Holy Smokes! You tore it up!! You had to be the most exciting player of the Blue Chip!"

Included in the bunch was a letter from Nebraska assistant coach Marty Everding:

Just wanted to send you a quick note to tell you that I saw you play over the weekend and was very impressed. A coaching friend of ours had pointed out to my Head Coach (John Walker) that, 'this girl is a Nebraska kind of player' and having now seen you play, I couldn't agree more. Your speed, ability and desire to go 1 v. 1, your physical toughness and ability in the air, and your overall competitiveness make you a very valuable player who I think would fit marvelously into our program.

Walker first saw Jenna play in June. It was a tournament in Indianapolis, and Jenna's Javanon club team was among those competing. Walker didn't have a roster or a program, but he found the field where Javanon was playing, and in an instant, he identified the future Husker. He was struck immediately by the electricity of her play.

"Within 5 minutes," Walker said, "she had tackled, sprinted, shot, yelled at her teammates to play harder and gotten into a skirmish with a much bigger opponent who eventually backed down from Jenna. I knew that I was looking at a future Nebraska captain."

Because there are only so many scholarships allowed per season for each Division I women's soccer program, most players receive a partial scholarship – maybe 25 percent or 50 percent. Jenna was considered worthy of a 100-percent scholarship.

Jenna visited Florida. The hometown school, Louisville, really wanted her to stay home. Notre Dame was also in the mix. But Jenna was interested in Nebraska's style of play, which was high-pressing, physical and relentless – an all-out attacking approach to the game. As Walker describes it, "a blur to play against."

Walker loved risk-takers, and Jenna fit the bill. She was about 5 feet 5 inches and a little more than 100 pounds, but she did not let her smallish size slow her daring style of play. The Husker coach was sold and returned to Louisville to get a commitment. He said he would meet Jenna at a Dairy Queen near her home on Northfield. She was running just a little late. Then suddenly a red Jeep comes zipping down the street and into the parking lot – kind of a blur. His future captain had arrived.

"When I went to visit her and Ellen, I found this incredibly sincere, humble, passionate person," Walker said. "The eyes always said it all. Full of life, passion, energy, fun."

Jenna knew that the risk-taking nature of Nebraska soccer was exactly what she wanted. She could have waited for Notre Dame to make her a strong offer or played it safe by choosing Louisville or Kentucky. But Jenna felt Nebraska was the place for her.

So in mid-August of 2001, William and Jenna loaded up a trailer and headed for Lincoln. After getting her settled into her place, William got ready to leave. He could tell that Jenna was not OK. There were a few tears, actually, which was unlike her. She was homesick in a heartbeat. Dad called work at the fiberglass plant and told them he would be missing a couple of days to stay with his girl. They hung out, visited Eagle Raceway – a dirt track near Lincoln – and the Speedway Motors racing museum and just passed the time until Jenna's new Husker teammates arrived. Once that happened, she felt at home right away, and Dad was good to go.

And any homesickness she felt didn't show on the soccer field. Jenna's first goal at Nebraska came on a long shot in an exhibition game against North Carolina, the top program in the nation. Not a bad way to start her collegiate career, and a sign of things to come. Most players would have gone crazy after scoring a goal against the Tar Heels. Jenna just headed back to the center circle like it was no big deal at all.

"In your first college game, you're playing the national champs with 2,500 people there, you get thrown in as a defender," Walker said. "She handled herself well. It didn't faze her one bit."

While she might not have shown a lot of emotion at the time, Jenna admitted it was an awesome experience.

"It was like a dream," she said, "especially against North Carolina."

Despite her relatively diminutive size, Jenna regularly mixed it up with much bigger opponents, but you could not keep her down. Walker could never remember Jenna missing a practice or a game because of an injury.

She played in all 70 Nebraska games over the course of her first three seasons in the program, starting 69 of those. She did not start against Southern Cal in the third game of her freshman season. Walker said she had performed poorly in practice in the week leading up to the game, and he had to bench her. However, she came out of that experience as determined as ever not to disappoint her coach or her teammates. She started every game from that point on and became an All-Big 12 Conference defender. She was invited to train with the United States national soccer program. Jenna had become exactly the kind of player that Walker had expected her to become when he saw her that day in Indianapolis.

In the classroom, Jenna was able to maintain better than a 3.0 grade point average while pursuing her degree in mechanical engineering. She worked hard and received help from tutors to keep her from slipping as a result of her focus issues. The academic support staff said her work ethic and drive allowed her to perform at a high level in school.

What most Nebraska fans didn't know was that Jenna would show up to the soccer complex early to help the folks in the concession stand get set up for that night's game. She was always there for teammates who needed some extra help on the field, or even if they just needed a ride to practice. She was always available when someone needed her.

Always improving, that was Jenna. Dave Griffiths, the coach who took over at Sacred Heart after Jenna graduated, told a great story about a 2-hour conversation he had with Jenna during Christmas break after her sophomore season.

"She wasn't just coming by to say 'Hi.' She wanted something," Griffiths said. "She told me, 'I want an edge. I want to play for the U.S. National Team.'"

They ended up talking for two hours, as Jenna shared her BFSB goal. She said she wanted to be Bigger, Faster, Stronger and Better.

From then on, every e-mail she sent to Griffiths ended with "BFSB, Jenna."

"I tell all the kids the same thing," Griffiths said. "If you've got an opportunity, you've got to take it. If you get half a chance, you've got to take it because you may not get the bloody chance again.

"I think she realized that."

In 2003, as a junior, Jenna had the finest season of her career. She was an all-conference defender who stepped up as a leader through the team's struggles – the most notable being a career-ending ACL injury suffered by captain Christy Harms.

Jenna went to Walker time after time, peeking her head into his office to ask what more she could do to help the team. When the season ended – with an NCAA second-round tournament loss at Portland – there was little doubt in the locker room about who the captain would be in 2004.

After the 2003 season, she knew it was time for her to step up, and she had a vision for the team as a whole doing the same.

BFSB

"When it comes to competitiveness, heart and guts," she said, "our team is probably No. 1 in the country, and we showed that this season."

The other Husker players gravitated to Jenna for a variety of reasons. For starters, she was just fun to be around, a young woman with a vibrant magnetism. But she was also a great player with an intense desire to be the best.

Jenna had not been chosen as captain by her coaches in high school, and that was sometimes hard for her to understand. She just didn't let on that it was a sore spot. When someone would ask if it bothered her, she would say, "As long as my cleats are on the field, I don't care."

Jenna led mostly by example – with her talent, toughness and intensity. Now, as the standout senior, it was time to lead in every way possible, as team captain. She received an early baptism into the role when Harms went down with an injury during the 2003 season.

"Going into next season," Jenna said, "I feel like I've already had a little of that (leadership) experience."

Jenna was OK with the responsibility and was willing to do whatever it took to be the field general the team needed. She would visit Coach Walker's office two or three times a week just to talk about leadership issues. She was a sponge for any nugget of guidance when it came to personal growth – on or off the soccer field. One guest speaker, former Nebraska volleyball coach Terry Pettit, talked to the soccer team about using the flock-of-geese leadership paradigm as its guide. Businesses have used the same model in management training.

Pettit shared these facts and lessons in a PowerPoint presentation to the team:

Fact 1: As each goose flaps its wings, it creates an "uplift" for the birds that follow. By flying in a "V" formation, the whole flock adds 71 percent greater flying range than if each bird flew alone.

Lesson: People who share a common direction and sense of community can get where they are going quicker and easier because they are traveling on the thrust of one another.

Fact 2: When a goose falls out of formation, it suddenly feels the drag and resistance of flying alone. It quickly moves back into formation to take advantage of the lifting power of the bird immediately in front of it.

Lesson: If we have as much sense as a goose, we stay in formation with those headed where we want to go. We are willing to accept their help and give our help to others.

Fact 3: When the lead goose tires, it rotates back into the formation and another goose flies to the point position.

Lesson: It pays to take turns doing the hard tasks and sharing leadership. As with geese, people are interdependent on each other's skills, capabilities and unique arrangements of gifts, talents or resources.

Fact 4: The geese flying in formation honk to encourage those up front to keep up their speed.

Lesson: We need to make sure honking is encouraging. In groups where there is encouragement the production is much greater. The power of encouragement (to stand by one's heart or core values and encourage the heart and core of others) is the quality of honking we seek.

Fact 5: When a goose gets sick, wounded or shot down, two geese drop out of formation and follow it down to help and protect it. They stay with it until it dies or is able to fly again. Then they launch out with another formation or catch up with the flock.

Lesson: If we have as much sense as geese, we will stand by each other in difficult times as well as when we are strong.

Not all of the Nebraska soccer players thought it was riveting training material, but Jenna, looking for any edge she could get, found it interesting. She thought about it. She talked about it. It was one more bit of enlightenment to file away. It suited her, this lesson. She was that someone who could fill any role – as devoted follower or as inspirational mentor.

Jenna knew it was time to be more of a leader.

"Going into next season," she said, "I feel like I've already had a little of that (leadership) experience."

Other players had already looked up to her, but now it was time to make it official. The girl who always wondered why she had never been chosen as captain in high school, was now the captain at Nebraska.

CHAPTER 4
Slaying Dragons

THE HONKING OF THE GEESE never left Wendy. She heard them, lots of them every fall as they did their fly-overs from Lake Michigan, over Luxemburg.

Wendy Peronto grew up there with two sisters and three brothers. They lived in the country, just outside of Green Bay. Their father, Al, worked for Wisconsin Public Service. Mom Joanne had a full-time job as a mother of six.

The kids loved to play in the woods. Wendy said they were just "a bunch of country hicks" having fun. Winters were spent on sleds and snowmobiles. Summer was for swimming. Wendy wasn't a star athlete, but she was a tomboy. She was a hurdler in junior high, but that was the extent of her athletic endeavors.

She loved horses, loved the outdoors, whether picking wildflowers or swimming in the pond on their land or wrestling with her brothers. She would hunt with them, too. She played drums in the band. She was not one to be intimidated.

Al bought the kids a horse when Wendy was about 8. It was a tan-and-white stallion named Dusty. Friends wondered what the heck Al was thinking buying the kids a wild horse like that. Dusty was not the easiest horse to handle, but right away, Wendy got on and went for a ride that appeared to be headed for disaster.

Dusty took off and went into a neighbor's yard, running like a horse possessed. But Wendy hung on, and Al was able to get Dusty back under control on the Peronto's property. Wendy was unharmed and seemingly unfazed by what looked like a darn scary ride for an 8-year-old.

"She was tough like that," Joanne said.

Sometimes, the family would visit the wildlife sanctuary in Green Bay to see the geese as they prepared for the trip south from Lake Michigan. In fall and winter, life in their hometown revolved around Packers football. Wendy wasn't a huge fan, but her dad sure was. And when she met Garth Davies, another Pack fanatic joined the clan.

Garth and Wendy first got to know each other at a popular Green Bay night spot called The Carlton West. They dated for several years before getting married in October of 1995. Luke was born on March 2, 2000, and Emily came along Feb. 23, 2003.

It was February, 2004, and the Davies were living in Luxemburg, just outside of Green Bay, when Wendy got terribly sick. Her heart started failing and she had to be airlifted to University of Wisconsin-Madison Hospital on February 28. She was there through April 18.

"I thought she was gone at least five times, maybe more," Garth said. She was in critical care, in and out of comas, dying of giant cell myocarditis, a rare disease with a wide range of symptoms.

Giant cell myocarditis most often occurs in young adults. Inflammation of the heart muscle is the key characteristic of the disease, and heart failure is often the end result. In Wendy's case, a heart transplant appeared to be the only hope for survival, but there were complications with that plan as well.

"I actually looked at the biopsy tissue myself and there was much more scar and inflammation there than there were heart muscle cells," said Dr. Maryl Johnson, Wendy's cardiologist.

She needed heart pumps, and so on March 2 she had surgery to have the bi-ventricular assist device installed. The BiVAD is two pumps each supporting one ventricle. In Wendy's case, it did not look like there was enough heart muscle for recovery. It was severely damaged by the inflammation. And at the time, she was even too sick to be put on a heart-transplant list because her other organs were struggling, too. There were so many questions about how long she would live, even with a new heart.

"By the time she was appropriate to be transplanted," Johnson said, "the tests that we had done showed that her body was making antibodies to a lot of other tissues, and so the word we use for that is 'sensitization,' and that means that many of the donors that would have become available, without specially treating Wendy, she would have rejected the heart immediately."

Wendy was in a coma for the week following the heart-pump surgery. She had internal bleeding. Doctors cut a hole in Wendy's ribs to insert a tube to drain blood. She had transfusion after transfusion. Garth said there were so many complications, it was hard to recall them all.

It was time to slay another dragon, and then another, and another. That is what Garth and Wendy talked about with each other and with their kids when their mom was sick – slaying dragons.

"The dragons show up," Garth said, "and you fight 'em off and you wait for the next one."

As hard as the Davies fought, the dragons were breathing a lot of fire. They were winning. Wendy was dying.

CHAPTER 5

No Quit

Jenna Cooper believed in luck. In fact, she often talked about how she thought she was the luckiest person on earth.

Friends would tell you she could spot a four-leaf clover a mile away, lots of them. Ali Malaekah, her club soccer coach and one of her biggest fans, said he would go back to his truck after practice and find bracelets and necklaces made of four-leaf clovers. How she found so many was a mystery.

Jenna was not a gambler, but before the spring soccer season started in 2004, Jenna and her brother took a weekend trip to Las Vegas with their Aunt Martina. One night at the Venetian, Jenna was having crazy good luck at the Black Jack table. Onlookers gathered around the pretty blonde. Who was this woman who was winning hand after hand? The spectators at Jenna's table – a $100 minimum table – started cheering for their new friend. By the end of the night, she was up about $20,000. An unbelievable night of good fortune for a Vegas novice. Luck on her side again.

Then things started to change. It wasn't long after that Vegas trip when Jenna called her parents in tears. She had been in a fender-bender, one in which she rear-ended another car. On the surface, it didn't seem like too big a deal, but the other driver was pretty upset and voiced her displeasure with plenty of anger. Jenna was really shaken by the incident. About the same time, she also found out that her roommate, Lindsey Ingram, was planning to move. Some bad karma was starting to take hold in Jenna, and she was not sure why. She told her parents she felt her luck was changing.

The last weekend of the spring soccer season began on a Friday night with Jenna providing the assist for Nebraska in a 1-1 tie with the Canadian National Team. Jenna made the pass that set up teammate Nikki Baker's game-tying goal for Nebraska. "Every day, I think about the huge smile on her face as I ran back to hug her," Baker said. "That smile was more than just soccer."

Jenna's mom was in the stands at the Abbott Sports Complex. She hadn't planned to be there for the exhibition game, but because Jenna was in the process of finding a new place to live, her mom decided to extend her visit to assist with the search.

As Jenna left the field that night, she made sure she showed her mom the tape around her wrist. The homemade bracelet was decorated with the No. 13, a reminder of a lost friend from Sacred Heart Academy. Lauren Tonini, a field hockey star, died in a car accident in September of 2003. Jenna and Lauren were both part of one of the top girls athletic programs in Kentucky – fellow Valkyries ("women warriors") of Sacred Heart.

That's how Jenna played soccer, like a warrior. Even in practice sessions, she set the pace for her teammates. Her last time on the soccer field – a work-out with the Canadian visitors on that Saturday morning – was no exception. If someone had told Jenna it was going to be her last time to play soccer, she wouldn't have played any harder. She couldn't have. It would have been impossible.

Her effort was particularly impressive when you consider how little sleep she got the night before. Jenna had to take her mom from Lincoln to Omaha – about a one-hour drive – to catch a 6:30 a.m. flight back to Louisville. She had been up since 4 a.m. Ellen didn't tell her daughter why she had to get back so early that day because she didn't want to add any stress to Jenna's weekend. The reason was a memorial event for Ellen's brother Doug. The family was dedicating a headstone. Uncle Doug, who had been paralyzed at age 17, was special to Jenna, which is why Ellen was careful not to bring it up, knowing Jenna had to stay in Lincoln that day for the final workout of the Huskers' spring season.

Jenna called her mom a couple of times on the drive back to Lincoln, making the final "I'm home OK" call as she picked up a cup of coffee at

McDonald's about 6 a.m. She told her mom not to worry. That she was fine. The caffeine would come in handy. The training session with the Canadians was far from a picnic. Team Canada coach Evan Pellerud was running the practice and really pushing the players. Everyone was struggling to catch their breath. Nebraska coach John Walker said Jenna held the practice together.

"Our team was tired from the game the night before," Walker said. "I remember the players were struggling. The one player who played great in that session was Jenna. Evan kept using her as an example. She had probably played 90 minutes or close to it the night before, and it was the next morning, and Evan was having them run, pretty much an all-out practice. She was just loving it."

Baker said Jenna was always pushing teammates to go the extra mile, to push a little harder. "I'll be the first to admit, some of us got annoyed with her at times because the girl never got tired. She never wanted to quit, and I never saw her giving less than her best."

But the hard work of the spring season was done. And that night, April 24, Jenna and Lindsey had a barbecue at their home to celebrate the end of spring practices. Jenna and Lindsey first met as freshmen, with Ingram coming to Nebraska from Littleton, Colo. They became close friends and lived together for about a year with their dogs – Jenna's miniature pincher, Dojah, and Lindsey's miniature dachshund, Dalby. The red ranch house they rented was in a quiet, family-filled neighborhood in southeast Lincoln, on 35th Street. The gathering was to be very casual, a time to cook out and have a few beers as a way to unwind after all those taxing workouts on the soccer field.

It was a typical social environment for college kids. The neighbors were accustomed to seeing parties at the house from time to time, but there had not been any complaints about disorderly or loud activity. Jenna and Lindsay, by all accounts, were good neighbors. And this party, by all accounts later, never caused any neighborhood disturbance.

Najah Williams, a former teammate and good friend, was staying at the house and helped get ready for the get-together. They bought chicken and corn and drinks, and Jenna would do the cooking. About 15 friends came over around 7 to have her Hawaiian Chicken and grilled corn-on-the-cob.

Jenna loved to cook for groups big and small, so she was having a great time entertaining and enjoying a few beers with her friends.

Several Husker soccer players, past and present, were there that night along with other friends of the two roommates. Jenna and some of the others talked about going out to the bars later, but Jenna thought it was best to stay put. She knew that driving was not an ideal option that night.

Some of the guests played a drinking game called Tippy Cup, a team relay in which you are supposed to flip a cup from the edge of a table so it lands upright. Jenna played, along with Lindsey and Lindsey's fiancée, Nolan Jenkins, and Najah and a few others. Everyone was having a great time. As the night progressed, word of the party spread, and more people started to arrive as bars started to close around 1 a.m.

One of the late arrivals was Lucky Iromuanya, a 22-year-old stranger to the group who heard about the gathering through his girlfriend, Maggie Rugh, who was at the party. Iromuanya arrived with a friend, Aroun Phaisan, shortly after midnight. It was at that time when Ingram noticed that Cooper's collection of shot glasses had disappeared. The shot glasses were a collection that Jenna had accumulated over the years, from road trips, usually soccer trips.

Ingram was not happy. She wanted to get to the bottom of the situation right away. There was tension. There was uncertainty. Throw in the fact that most of the people involved had been drinking, and you had a recipe for trouble. As tense as it was, no one could have foreseen the tragic path the night was about to take.

Another latecomer to the party was Jared Predmore, a college student who learned about the party from Nate Buss, another student who practiced with the soccer team. They also arrived between midnight and 12:30. It was Predmore who took the shot glasses. "That's not cool," Buss told Predmore. "This is one of my friend's houses. That's not cool at all."

Predmore had put the glasses in Buss' car. Buss told Ingram someone had taken the glasses but he wasn't sure who it was. He also told Cooper, but again without sharing more about who did it. Buss thought he could get the shot glasses back without any kind of confrontation and without singling out his friend.

But tempers were starting to flare, regardless of who was responsible, and Ingram was not going to let anyone leave the home until she figured out where the glasses had gone. She confronted Predmore and two of his friends in the living room, and Predmore admitted that he took the glasses. Predmore and Ingram then walked to Buss's car to reclaim Jenna's property. But when she saw Iromuanya and Phaisain walking away from the house quickly, she wondered if they had anything to do with the situation. She had also been told by Predmore that "friends" told him to take the glasses, so she wanted to know if others were involved, possibly Iromuanya and Phaisain.

While walking with Predmore, she yelled for no one to leave the house. It started to get more heated, and Jenkins and Iromuanya began to scuffle. Jenkins thought Iromuanya had been the one who took Jenna's shot glasses.

Ingram went back to tell Jenkins what she had discovered and that it was not Iromuanya, but blood was already boiling. The combination of alcohol and adrenaline had taken over. She told Iromuanya to "chill out" before going back inside. Jenna and Brooke Bredenberg, were among those trying to calm everyone down. Jenna approached Iromuanya to tell him everything was OK. She extended a hand. "I'm touching you. I'm touching you," she said in an attempt to relax him.

Iromuanya was still upset. Jenkins was still upset. And shortly after 2 a.m., Ingram, from the living room, heard a gunshot and screams from the front yard. The pop came from a .32-caliber Derringer fired by Iromuanya. The bullet grazed Jenkins' skull and ended up striking Jenna standing 20 feet away.

Iromuanya and Phaisan took off, driving away quickly in Phaisan's SUV. Jenkins was dazed and bleeding. Jenna was on the ground. Ingram, a nursing student, saw blood on Jenna's shoulder and head but did not see anything to indicate it was a life-threatening wound.

The first calls were to 911. The next to Kentucky.

CHAPTER 6

The Hardest Goodbye

ELLEN COOPER WAS ASLEEP AT home in Louisville when the phone rang at about 3 a.m., less than 24 hours after she and Jenna had made the trip to the Omaha airport. Few of those types of calls in the middle of the night are good. This was one was more horrible than any parent could imagine.

It was Ingram calling to tell Ellen that Jenna had been shot in the shoulder.

"She knew it wasn't OK," said Jenna's brother, Billy, who was living at home at the time.

When paramedics tore apart Cooper's shirt, the severity of the situation became clear. The deflected bullet had hit Cooper in the throat. It had damaged her carotid artery and lodged in her lung.

Ellen, Billy and Jenna's father, William, started their trip to Nebraska with a flight to Atlanta. On that flight, Ellen had a feeling she already had lost her girl.

"Jenna just died. Jenna just died."

As the family waited for a connecting flight, doctors told Ellen by phone that Jenna had coded. It would have been about the time Ellen had that awful feeling that Jenna had died. But for the moment, things were stabilizing. The physician reported that Jenna was again showing signs of life.

Walker also got a call about 3 a.m., and he immediately notified Steve Pederson, the athletic director at Nebraska. Early media reports that morning indicated that a Nebraska soccer player had been shot, and that someone was in custody as the prime suspect, but there were no details about the identity of the victim.

Ellen, William and Billy made it to Lincoln about 1 p.m. They found a hospital full of Jenna's biggest fans and supporters and protectors of the heart.

Jenna would have marveled at the number of people who came to stay with her and pray for her, but she would have been upset by all the fuss. She never craved attention but always attracted crowds.

After Jenna's freshman season at Nebraska, in 2001, she had returned home for Christmas break to find about 30 people at the airport, some holding signs and balloons, to welcome back their Husker star for the holidays. Jenna appreciated the big greeting but also felt so embarrassed by the whole thing that she vowed never again to announce a specific return time on future trips home.

But the fact was, lots of people loved Jenna, and they followed her. She thought it was important to be an organ donor, so when she signed her new driver's license as a sophomore at Sacred Heart Academy, others followed.

When her high school and college teammates wanted to see how the game of soccer should be played, they looked to Jenna. When little Husker fans wanted some words of encouragement and an autograph from a star, they ran to Jenna.

So it was no wonder so many family members and friends came to the hospital to make sure that undeniable smile was going to be safe, the smile that would not go away.

Jenna couldn't frown without intense effort. Her friends talked about how the little soccer bug from Louisville couldn't make a pouty face. Her facial muscles wouldn't allow it. She would crack them up by trying to make a sad face, but she couldn't. Don't be sad. That was the rule, plain and simple, even on the most horrible day.

Jenna's condition was considered 'critical to grave,' according to Dr. Reginald Burton, the trauma surgeon who was in charge of her care. It was a very unstable situation, and Jenna's blood pressure was at a dangerous low. Dr. Burton could tell quickly that it was going to be a complicated case because of where the injury was located. The bullet had gone through the neck, through the upper part of her shoulder, and it was lying just inside of her shoulder blade on the right side. It had struck the innominate artery, a very tough vessel for surgical repair because the only way to expose is through the chest.

The innominate (brachiocephalic) artery is on the right side of the body and is the first branch off the aortic arch as it leaves the heart. It is only a couple of millimeters in diameter. The odds of the bullet striking the vessel were astronomical, but that is what happened.

Chest tubes were used to drain blood from outside of the lung, and while there were many complications, the vessel was repaired, and the team in the O.R. started to feel optimistic about Jenna's recovery, in no small part because of her strength and young age. Dr. Burton said they thought she might be OK.

Megan Skinner remembered seeing some positive signs that afternoon. She said everyone believed, without a doubt, that Jenna was going to make it. She was such a fighter, all 5-foot-5 of her. She once finished a soccer practice with a broken arm.

One of the main reasons Walker wanted her as a Husker was her willingness to mix it up with bigger opponents, her fearlessness.

"She would get tossed around like a rag doll sometimes," said Nebraska teammate Iman Haynes, "and she would pop right back up."

But things turned dark again late in the afternoon because of poor blood flow through vessels to the head. That led to swelling of the brain, and that was just part of the battle, as the ER team hand-massaged Jenna's heart to keep it pumping.

When family members arrived at the hospital, they were told to speak to Jenna in a loud tone, to try to get her to respond in any way possible.

"When we got there, the doctors said she was stable, and they wanted us to try to wake her up," William said.

The injuries had hindered the flow of oxygen to the brain at various times during the ordeal, so the threat of long-term brain damage was very real.

"It was incredibly difficult to walk in and see that," William said. "So we tried to hold her hand and talk to her."

Jenna's mom kept calling to her, asking her to wake up. Jenna was responsive. She squeezed her mom's hand. She raised her left leg briefly, that magic left leg that had done so much on soccer fields from Kentucky to Nebraska and beyond.

Then something even more remarkable happened. Tears started to form in Jenna's eyes. It was a sight that Ellen could not have imagined. All Jenna's mom could think about at that moment was how rare it was for Jenna to cry. Tears were not part of her makeup because she always believed they were a sign of weakness.

But whether she was aware of the situation or not, her mom felt this was a sign that she knew it might be time to say goodbye. So much of her was broken, and now some of the thousands of tears being shed all around that hospital were hers.

The doctors decided it was best for Jenna to be left alone as they monitored her status. Her blood pressure readings were not good, but the believers outside that room were convinced she would get through this. She was too strong to let it end.

All day and into Sunday evening, her fan club sat and waited, standing guard. It was going to be OK. But as evening approached, it became clear to everyone that Jenna was in trouble. They wheeled Jenna's body by, and all you could see was her head and her feet. That wavy blonde hair and those remarkable feet, one of which had been referred to by an admirer as the Left Foot of God.

The foot could make the soccer ball do wonderful things, amazing things. Corner kicks. Free kicks. Penalty kicks. Short, precise passes. Long serves. Jenna was part of the U.S. national program for a reason. She was that good. Skinner thought about how those feet were such a special part of Jenna.

When she heard medical personnel talking of organ donation, Skinner's first instinct was that Jenna needed a transplant to survive. The coach thought, "OK, let's line up and get tested to be a match for whatever organs she needs." That wasn't what was happening, though.

William and Billy were outside trying to get some fresh air, but they were told they needed to get back inside. Jenna was being rushed back to the emergency room.

"The doctor came up and kind of mapped it out. He said it was the worst-case scenario," William said. "He explained to us that she wasn't going to survive."

The doctors were accompanied by police officers and sheriff's deputies.

"At that time, they couldn't harvest Jenna's organs because she was considered to be evidence," William said. "That's the way it was. They had to get a court order to allow them to remove her organs."

The doctors were suggesting that family members say their goodbyes to Jenna. Ellen asked her friends and teammates if they wanted to see her one last time. Some did. Others could not. Jenkins, who was hurting but alert, was among the visitors.

Legal paperwork was completed so Jenna's organs could be harvested Monday. As Ellen recalled the discussion, doctors said they weren't sure if her heart would be strong enough to survive a transplant because of Jenna's smallish size and young age.

The idea that Jenna's heart was not big enough, not strong enough did not seem possible, but the doctors needed to know how to proceed.

Jenna's wishes were to give those organs away, not to science or a medical school, but to someone in need right then and now. She even wrote down her request on an "affirmation of life" worksheet during her senior year at Sacred Heart:

I would not want to be put on life support in any case unless to preserve organs for donation.

And she wouldn't want a fuss about any of it. No fuss. That was Jenna from the time she was a baby. She was not the kind of infant to need a marathon rocking session to go to sleep. Her grandmother, Pat McLaughlin, said Jenna wanted you to put her in the crib and be done with it. Leave her be and go.

Life support was stopped.

Jenna Marie Cooper died at 7:21 p.m., April 25, 2004.

She was gone. Jenna was really gone. The darkness of it was unfathomable, and there were no cans of spray paint to make it all seem better.

Ellen had just been with her daughter the day before. Not in her wildest, most horrible dreams could she have imagined that it would be the last time they would share a laugh or a conversation together.

Ellen and William tried to keep up a brave face because there were so many arrangements that needed to be made. Many family members stayed at the same downtown hotel. Ellen shared a room with her mother and sister Sandy. Ellen had been trying so hard to not let the pain show, but the time came to let it all go. She dropped to her knees and begged God to take her, too. She didn't want to live a minute apart from Jenna. She cried all night.

William returned to the downtown hotel where many family members were staying, and with the news of his daughter's death on many of the television stations, he turned to American Chopper for a futile attempt at distraction.

In trying to find a way to deal with the pain, Billy Cooper and a few of Jenna's friends and teammates went out after midnight to the soccer practice field on the Nebraska campus. One of her best friends, Brooke Bredenberg, knew how to turn on the lights, so off they went, kicking the ball around into the wee hours of the morning. It was one way to honor Jenna and to let her know that everyone was going to do their best to cope.

Jenna was gone, but not her spirit and not her heart.

CHAPTER 7

Still the Captain

LUCKY IROMUANYA WAS LOCATED AT home quickly after the shooting and charged with second-degree murder. Jenna's death was a major news story – the top news story in the state for several days.

She died on a Sunday night, and on that Monday, John Walker and a few of the players who were closest to Jenna met with the media to talk about her death.

The Nebraska soccer program was not accustomed to a lot of media attention. The school newspaper – the Daily Nebraskan – the Lincoln Journal Star and the Omaha World-Herald staffed most of the team's home games, but NU soccer was way down on the media priority list because of the intense interest in Husker football and volleyball at that time of year. The local TV stations would occasionally show highlights from home soccer games, but that would be no more than 20 seconds or so at a clip.

But on the Monday afternoon after Jenna's death, the room used for team meetings was packed with reporters and cameras.

Lindsey Ingram brought a prop to the news conference – a pair of big, black sunglasses that Jenna used to wear to lighten up the locker room. They came with frames that would have made Harry Caray proud.

Just down the hall from that room was a door with a sign-up sheet for players who wanted to help with the team's youth soccer camps over the summer. Jenna had signed up for several sessions.

On Tuesday, the university held a memorial service on one of the club levels of the football stadium. It was a big room used for special events for Husker boosters. It was filled. They put a picture of Jenna up on the scoreboard during the service. Coaches and athletes from all sports attended along with many people who had watched her play as Nebraska soccer fans.

From the Lincoln Journal Star:

Lindsey Ingram and Jenna Cooper, two sparkplugs not much bigger than 10 feet tall combined, were roommates who were known to their teammates as the "Twin Towers."

But with her best friend gone, Ingram had to be the tower of strength Tuesday afternoon as she spoke to friends, fellow Huskers and the Cooper family during a one-hour service at Memorial Stadium.

"Her extraordinary beauty awed all of us," Ingram said. "I have to admit that every time someone would mistake me for her, I was honored."

With Jenna Cooper's smile shining brightly on the HuskerVision screens overlooking the football field, the stadium's third-floor club level was packed with close to 1,000 supporters. They came to say goodbye to the soccer team captain, who died of a gunshot wound Sunday night at the age of 21.

The crowd included student-athletes and coaches from all walks of Husker athletics. Among them were former NU soccer stars Meghan Anderson, Breanna Boyd, Christine Latham and Kori Saunders.

Members of the Nebraska baseball and softball were present, just a couple of hours before they were scheduled to compete at Haymarket Park. New head football coach Bill Callahan was there, and so was Saunders' father, Kansas City Chiefs offensive coordinator Al Saunders.

Some wore red ribbons decorated with Cooper's No. 3. Others wore green ribbon pins, a symbol to promote organ donation. Cooper's organs will be used to help save lives.

Ingram came dressed in one of Cooper's Husker jerseys. She fought through an upbeat but tearful eulogy with teammate Kari Hogan and former Husker Najah Williams by her side.

"Her friendship is truly one in a million," Ingram said.

NU head soccer coach John Walker presented Cooper's mother, Ellen, with one of her daughter's jerseys.

"There was no other place she wanted to go (besides NU)," said Ellen Cooper, who was seated in front with Jenna's father, William, Jenna's brother, Billy, and several other family members from their hometown – Louisville, Ky.

Ellen said Jenna's teammates told the family Sunday, as Jenna hung on in a bed at Bryan LGH Medical Center West, that it was time to pray for a miracle.

"I told them, 'We had a miracle for 21 years,'" Ellen Cooper said.

Athletic director Steve Pederson provided the words of welcome Tuesday, commending Cooper's parents for her upbringing.

"Congratulations on raising a daughter who made Nebraska a better place," Pederson said. "There are now hundreds of young soccer players who want to be Jenna Cooper someday."

Walker described Cooper as someone extraordinary "who went out of her way to try to make herself seem average."

"She was the ultimate teammate," he said.

Walker joked about how Cooper loved to cruise around town in her red jeep and about how she strived to make sure the Huskers were a "kick-ass type of team."

He said he knew Cooper, a graduate of Sacred Heart Academy in Louisville, was Big Red material as soon as he saw her play.

"I saw this skinny, left-footed kid in an altercation with a much bigger opponent," he said. "I thought, 'She's got to be a Husker.'"

Dr. John Ballard, dean of the College of Engineering and Technology, spoke after Walker, describing Cooper's excellence in her field of study – mechanical engineering.

"I'm confident she would have succeeded as a mechanical engineer the same way she succeeded on the soccer field," Ballard said.

According to Ingram, Cooper's mechanical expertise often came in handy around the house.

"She made sure the cars ran," Ingram said. "And she was my fashion consultant."

The service ended with a highlight video of Cooper's Husker career set to Diamond Rio's "One More Day."

Most of those in attendance were connected with the Nebraska athletic department or the Cooper family. But Husker fan Lance McCord of Lincoln just wanted to be there with his three young soccer players – Wesley, 11; Anna, 8; and Jackson, 5 – to offer some comfort from a distance.

"I just thought I'd come down and show support for the family," he said.

Many of those who attended Tuesday were expected to travel to Louisville for a service Friday.

Husker assistant soccer coach Marty Everding said the past couple of days have been a struggle. The struggle will continue, with different members of the team dealing with the loss in different ways.

"For all of us, the tsunami is at different places," he said. "For Lindsey, it's crashed. For others, it's still out there in the middle of the ocean. It's still out there, but it's coming."

The Huskers will need Cooper's strength now, more than ever.

"I've told our team," Walker said during his eulogy, "the only appropriate way to honor her is to carry on the way she would have wanted.

"She's still the captain."

On that day, Walker also talked about how Jenna would look after his young daughter on road trips. He talked about how she would always bounce back up after taking a knock (or delivering one) on the soccer field. He talked about her spirit, and how it provided such a lift to the people around her.

"Can you imagine having the charisma to make heaven a better place?" Walker asked. "I have no doubt that this has happened already."

The team then traveled to Louisville for a service in Jenna's hometown. The Cathedral of the Assumption was filled with thousands of mourners. Jenna's teammates wore their Nebraska soccer uniforms for the service and lined the walkway between pews as the casket was carried past.

Jenna's body was taken to the family cemetery, a secluded area in the woods. Because of heavy rains, it was a muddy trip to get the casket to the burial site. Pallbearers were getting splattered with mud, which added much-needed levity to the situation.

"We had a four-wheel drive vehicle with a trailer for the casket," William Cooper said. "Six pallbearers sat on the trailer. It was really bad. At one time, we got real close to the cemetery. The thing jack-knifed and we hit a tree. We tried to give it all the gas. Ali (Malaekeh), who was on the corner of the trailer, had a three-piece suit on, and got totally covered with mud.

"We started laughing because that was Jenna. She loved mud. The slippier the better."

Just like the day she fell in love with soccer on her dad's front lawn.

The Coopers received hundreds of letters and e-mails of support and sympathy, including dozens and dozens from people she didn't know.

"She had an amazing heart," wrote one of Jenna's classmates at Sacred Heart Academy in Louisville, "and you could see such radiance of life in her eyes."

Ali, Jenna's club soccer coach with the Javanon 83s, wrote: "Her drive to improve fueled the competitive fire of the team. Her love for her teammates was the glue that kept everything together in good times and hard times. I miss her smile, her sense of humor, her competitiveness, the e-mails and instant messages and most of all, her friendship."

One of her favorite times of year was Kentucky Derby time, the first Saturday in May every year. Jenna always told her friends in Nebraska that they needed to get to Churchill Downs for Derby week just once in their lives. It just so happened that the race was just a day after Jenna's memorial service in Louisville. Some of those friends decided it was finally time to see the Derby for themselves – for Jenna.

"She always talked about Kentucky and how beautiful it was," Bredenberg said.

So they headed to the track on that rainy Saturday. As the feature race approached, the sun started to peek through and the group there for Jenna was given a chance to stand right by the track in one of the high-dollar seating areas. They paid $10 for the right to sit in $1,000 seats.

Jenna wore No. 15 while competing for Sacred Heart Academy in high school, and No. 3 at Nebraska, so her friends decided to wager on No. 15 (Smarty Jones) and No. 3 (Lion Heart) in the Kentucky Derby. It was the first time any of them had bet on a horse race.

"No. 3 was leading," said Bredenberg, "and then, all of a sudden, 15 comes up, and we're like 'No way.'"

There came No. 15 Smarty Jones, with jockey Stewart Elliott wearing blue silks with a giant C on the chest. It did not stand for Cooper, but why not pretend? No. 15 was winning for real.

Jenna wore No. 3 at Nebraska as a tribute to Dale Earnhardt and because No. 15 was taken by Husker goalkeeper Erin Miller when Jenna joined the program.

There was no doubt that 15 was her first love. She even wrote about it in a school paper at Sacred Heart.

When my brother quit playing soccer in high school I took his number 15. I've stuck with it for 7 years now. It's become my lucky number. When I got my license plate for my car my dad called me and told me I had to come check it out. He seemed really excited about this license plate for some reason. So I went over and took a look at it, sure enough it was labeled "1515 DT." I asked him how he ordered it like that and he told me that he didn't order it, that it just came that way. I was so surprised, but it was awesome.

So was the finish of the 130th running of the Kentucky Derby, with No. 15 Smarty Jones first and No. 3 Lion Heart second. It is the only time in the history of the famous race that those two numbers have come in first and second.

Many of Jenna's friends have saved copies of this postcard of the race,
showing Smarty Jones and Lion Heart running together down the stretch.
Jenna's dad has a large picture of the finish hanging in his bedroom.
"That has so much meaning to me," William Cooper said. "It's incredible."
(Photo Copyright Kinetic Corporation Churchill Downs, Inc.)

CHAPTER 8

A Really Good Heart

WINTERS IN GREEN BAY ARE not for the weak of heart. They pack a chill that grabs you in October and doesn't let go until April. The community's work ethic can be seen in the giant smoke clouds floating over the paper mills along the Fox River, not far from legendary Lambeau Field. Green Bay has an amazing love affair with its Packers, but when football season is over, the wait for spring can be brutal.

The cold of winter 2004 had been especially stifling for the Davies family. From late February on, there was fear and pain and great concern over Wendy's health. The dragons kept coming and coming, and the feeling was miserable. The thought of eating made her nauseous. Every bite was a chore. She could not sleep on her side because of the bi-ventricular assist device (BIVAD) and all the body attachments that were keeping the blood flowing. Wendy would have given anything for a hot shower, but even that simple part of most people's daily routine was not possible. She could not stay warm. The cold was constant.

"That's something that people commonly say," said Wendy's cardiologist, Maryl Johnson, "because when the heart is not pumping properly our peripheral blood vessels constrict trying to maintain circulation to the brain and the heart and the other vital organs and the periphery really doesn't get as much blood flow."

The only solution was the warmth that would come with a new heart, and all the Davies could do was wait for the call that one was on its way. They waited for weeks.

At about 3 a.m. on Monday, April 26, Wendy was awake and thirsty. She asked for some juice. The nurse said "no, no Wendy, you can't have juice. You might be getting a new heart."

You might be getting a new heart.

After almost two months of waiting and knowing that time was short, prayers were being answered in Wisconsin. Through the United Network of Organ Sharing, a donor heart in Lincoln, Nebraska, was deemed suitable for Wendy.

Take the excitement of the Packers winning a Super Bowl times 100 and it couldn't compare to the excitement in that hospital room. Wendy started calling relatives to tell them the great news, although she knew nothing about the story behind this gift.

The process and procedure that made it possible is no simple thing. A lot has to fall into place for a good heart-donor match. It starts with the Organ Procurement and Transplantation Network (OPTN), which is a computer network connecting all organ procurement and transplant centers around the country.

Wendy's transplant center was UW Hospital in Madison. That is where tests were run to make sure she was a good candidate for a transplant. She was placed on the UNOS waiting list.

When a deceased organ donor is identified, a transplant coordinator from an organ procurement organization accesses the UNOS computer. Each patient in the database is matched by the computer against the donor characteristics. The computer then generates a ranked list of candidates for each available organ in ranked order according to OPTN organ allocation policies.

The match for each donor organ is different depending on a number of factors – tissue match, blood type, length of time on the waiting list, immune status and the distance between the potential recipient and the donor. The organ is offered to the transplant team for the first person on the match list.

Often, the top patient will not get the organ for one of several reasons. The potential recipient must be healthy enough to have major surgery immediately. And there can be other obstacles as well. For example, patients with high antibody levels often prove incompatible to the donor organ and cannot receive the organ because the patient's immune system would reject it. Once a patient is selected and contacted and all testing is complete, surgery is scheduled and the transplant takes place.

The transplant needed to take place right away in Wendy's case. She had been having mini-strokes and complications with her BIVAD. Dr. Johnson said there was also concern about a situation with an antibody response to the heparin that she was being given.

"We were concerned," Johnson said, "that she could have a big stroke."

But the transplant, completed at about noon, went very smoothly. The heart was close to perfect for Wendy. And that was no small thing, given the circumstances of Jenna Cooper's death.

"People that die traumatic deaths, as most donors do, certainly can have some heart muscle dysfunction," Johnson said, "because of the hormonal things that happen around the time of death."

But this heart was strong, and after the transplant, Wendy woke up with a big smile on her face, and she woke to a greeting from her anesthesiologist.

"Congratulations, you have a new heart."

She could feel a warmth she had not felt in months. No more extra blankets.

"They gave me a good heart," she said, "a really good heart."

A superstar heart.

Jenna had joined the dragon slayers in Wisconsin, and it was nothing short of miraculous.

Wendy was better, just like that. She could eat what she wanted again. She could wear her favorite clothes again. She could take a hot shower and sleep on her side again.

"How do you explain it," she said, "when you're half-dead and then you're alive?"

Wendy said before she woke up, she remembered seeing "a ton of people praying for me."

What people?

"I remember seeing people around me in white gowns, and they were comforting me, and they were relaxing me. They would all go around the bed and do something to comfort me.

"Whether they were angels, I don't know."

CHAPTER 9

Jenna's Team

THERE ARE NATURAL BORN LEADERS, and there are those who are willing to lead but are somewhat reluctant in the role. They do the job because the job must be done. That was Jenna Cooper, a little hesitant to take charge at first but willing all the same.

After Jenna's death, the Husker flock had to turn to the other veterans on the team, starting with seniors-to-be Brooke Bredenberg, Iman Haynes and Lindsey Ingram. Because Haynes was injured, Bredenberg and Ingram knew they were going to have to take the lead with the help of some of the other more experienced players.

To prepare for what everyone knew would be an extremely difficult season – emotionally and physically – the team spent the first week of pre-season camp in Nebraska City, a small town along the Missouri River, just across from Iowa. They gathered at a camp site mostly used for Girls Scout retreats. The soccer fields weren't in the best of shape, but the team didn't really go there to work on soccer. They went there to try to heal a painful heartbreak.

The place had a big restaurant style kitchen – Jenna would have loved it – and different classes took turns preparing the meals for the team – freshmen one night, sophomores the next and so on. Evenings were filled with movies, casual conversation and S'mores by the campfire.

There were no outside distractions except for a reporter and a photographer from Sports Illustrated On Campus who were allowed to spend some time with the team. Walker thought it would be OK to allow the journalists into the retreat for a short time because he thought it might help get Jenna's story out there for a larger audience.

All in all, the results of the Nebraska City retreat were positive. The players needed the chance to spend some alone time with those who really knew the pain of the tragedy, and the camp served that purpose well, regardless of what was accomplished on the practice field.

But then it was time to really get back to work in Lincoln. Numbers were thin on the Nebraska roster. Jenna's loss obviously was the most painful, in many ways, but several other players were out because of injuries. And some of the team's stars were away competing for the Canadian national team in the Olympics. The team was so lean of bodies, Walker held open tryouts for all comers on campus, anyone with the skills to compete at the collegiate level.

In August, on a muggy Saturday night, the team held a ceremony to retire Jenna's No. 3 festivities, which took place before the team's alumni reunion game. Walker told the crowd that "every player who comes to Nebraska will know the story of Jenna Cooper." Ingram said the team would continue "to dream Jenna's lofty dreams."

Just as Jenna's jersey was officially retired, a perfect formation of Canada geese flew overhead, right overhead, not more than a few feet above the festivities. At that moment, an awed silence created an unplanned pause in the ceremonies. Spectators turned to each other with the same question: "Did you see that?"

"It was incredible," William Cooper said. "It was almost eerie the way they flew down and just cruised over the field. It seemed odd during a sporting event that they would even do that, with all the lights and everything there."

It would be hard to imagine a more appropriate sign from above that Jenna was still there with the team. But it was also another sign that the geese, with different leaders taking their turns at the front of the formation. No. 3 was not with the Huskers physically, but she was without a doubt the presence her teammates would turn to the most in 2004.

Assistant coach Megan Skinner said the team's expectations for the season were not related to wins and losses. The expectations were related to Jenna.

"Would she be proud of our effort? Is that how she would have led?" The coaches knew there would be days when they couldn't be as hard on the team in practice. They knew that it might only take one wrong word or action to send emotions spiraling.

"The one thing I know that kept many of us going," Skinner said, "was the fact we were going to be back in Louisville for a memorial game early in the summer."

And from that inspiration came a strong start to the season. The Huskers held their own despite the thin roster. They played No. 1 North Carolina very tough in a 1-0 loss to open the season. A near-record crowd of 3,650 came out to support the Huskers, who hung with the Tar Heels despite being outshot 18-3. Nebraska started the year with a 10-3 record and eventually climbed into the national rankings on Sept. 28, Jenna's birthday.

Things were going well for the team despite the negative fallout from the Sports Illustrated story. Players and coaches were upset that the piece was published as more of a detailed description of the shooting than a story about Jenna's life. The cover of the magazine was done in black and white with the bold headline: "The Nebraska Murder." The team felt betrayed. It was not the story they had hoped for. It was just more damage from which to recover.

Signs of Jenna were everywhere. Players penned the word "Coop" on their cleats. Lockers were decorated with photos and other mementos connected to Jenna. During the national anthem before games, the team left a space for No. 3 in the line of players holding hands. Jenna took the anthem seriously. If teammates were goofing around during the Star Spangled Banner, she would tell them to knock it off in not-so-subtle terms.

With Jenna gone, the Senior Night game in 2004 was especially difficult. The Huskers were emotionally spent and played with little energy in a 2-0 loss to Colorado. The following week, the Huskers lost to Texas in the first round of the Big 12 Tournament.

Three straight losses had Nebraska sputtering into the NCAA Tournament. The Huskers had made it to the third round of the NCAA championship – the Sweet 16 – in seven of the last eight seasons, but doing it in 2004 seemed extremely unlikely, especially with star players Brittany Timko and Tanya Dennis out of the country competing with the Canadian national team.

It did not appear the team had enough gas left in the red Jeep to go anywhere in the NCAA Tournament, but they received a bid in the field of 64 and were sent to play in Lawrence, Kan., for a first-round game against Oral Roberts. The Huskers took care of business in the opening game with a 3-0 victory, setting up a second-round showdown with conference rival Kansas.

Although Nebraska defeated Kansas 1-0 earlier in the season, the rematch looked like a mismatch. The Jayhawks were 18-4 and rated as the No. 8 team in the country. Their roster was large in numbers and loaded with all-conference performers, including goalkeeper Meghan Miller.

Nebraska was 13-8 and unranked, but the biggest concern for Walker was his lack of team depth against such a strong team. Before the Kansas game, he met with seven key players – Sasha Andrews, Nikki Baker, Brooke Bredenberg, Katie Bunkers, Vern Fitzgerald, Lindsey Ingram and Aly Scace.

Walker made it clear that those players, the most experienced on the team, would have to step up for the Huskers to have a chance against the Jayhawks.

Walker talked about Jenna before the game, about how she would have loved to have been out there for that Sunday afternoon tussle in Lawrence. He told the team they had a chance to do something special despite the long odds. This was a team that could have used every excuse in the book. They were short-handed. They were tired. They were heartbroken. But Walker reminded the Huskers that this was Jenna's team.

Walker had not used Jenna's death in pre-game talks during the season. He said it was something that he didn't want to use as a cheap gimmick to fire up the team. But he did say early in the season that he would mention Jenna and her spirit when he deemed it appropriate.

This was the time. Skinner said it was one of Walker's finest moments.

"He made one of the most inspirational pre-game talks," she said. "John concluded by simply saying, 'the No. 3 has always been a major part of our season and that today we needed to think of Jenna and play as if she is on the field with us.'

He mentioned three things that the Huskers would need to prevail.

Play with your minds first.
Play with your physical skills.
Play with your hearts.

If they played together, for Jenna, and if they played to the end, they would have a chance. The Huskers played well from the opening kick and took a 1-0 lead 27 minutes into the game. The goal came on a free kick from Bredenberg, who bent a perfect shot over a wall of players, off the hand of goalkeeper Meghan Miller and into the left side of the net.

Bredenberg, one of Jenna's closest friends, was always working on free kicks even when she was not the player designated to take them. That was Jenna's job. Jenna used to work on the kicks with Meghan Anderson, a star player who was a mentor to Jenna early in her career. And then it was Bredenberg and Jenna working after practice on those free kicks, how to make the ball go this way or that way, in any situation.

Jenna didn't know she was training her successor, and Bredenberg had no reason to believe that she would ever need those skills in a game. Some of the Huskers used to wonder why Bredenberg spent so much time working on free kicks when she was not the player who would be asked to take them.

There was a reason.

"She's out there every day, before and after practice," Walker said. "Every single day, and you do it for that one moment. One moment. Today was the moment."

Bredenberg's goal put the Huskers ahead, but there was a lot of soccer left to be played. At halftime, Walker asked the team to play as hard as possible for the first 15 minutes and then just try to hold on with solid defense at the finish.

The second half was all Kansas. The Jayhawks outshot the Huskers 17-1. Yes, 17 to 1. KU peppered sophomore goalkeeper Katie Wright with a variety of attacks. However, the only shot that got past Wright came from Jessica Smith at 67:52. Despite the barrage of scoring chances from Kansas, Nebraska kept it tied after 90 minutes. It was not just the work of Bredenberg and Ingram and the older players, either.

Sophomore Abby Penas, normally a forward, held her own while playing left back. Freshmen Meghan Hungerford and Brigid Kenny filled in admirably when called upon. Junior Kari Hogan, one of the players most devastated by Jenna's death, also played with the strength and toughness of her lost friend.

But it was pretty clear that the Huskers were just barely hanging on when regulation time expired. They prepared for overtime with almost nothing left to expend. Kansas could have played with eight or nine and would have still been considered the favorite to win in sudden death.

Kansas head coach Mark Francis said the Huskers, "basically were done. They were tired. They were on their heels a little bit… We were all over them."

Fact 5: When a goose gets sick, wounded or shot down, two geese drop out of formation and follow it down to help and protect it. They stay with it until it dies or is able to fly again. Then they launch out with another formation or catch up with the flock.

Lesson: If we have as much sense as geese, we will stand by each other in difficult times as well as when we are strong.

There is no sitting back on your heels in overtime. Not when the first goal determines the winner. Nebraska would have to try to score quickly, or they would have no chance to hold off the Jayhawks. With exhaustion taking its toll, Walker knew his team would not survive a long overtime period.

But as tired as they were, the Huskers were calm and composed in the tension of the moment. Nebraska had so little left, but it had No. 3. There were 12 Huskers on that field in overtime.

"I think one thing they carry over from Jenna, on the field," Walker said, "there's not a lot of panic."

About 4 minutes in, Penas sent a pass toward Baker in the midfield area. Baker maneuvered to get into an open space, and from about 30 feet out, she blasted a left-footed rocket of a shot toward Miller and the Kansas goal. Baker's blast hit the bottom of the crossbar and bounced into the net, touching off as wild a celebration as you'll ever see on a soccer pitch.

"I don't know how she made that goal," Bredenberg said. "It was the most difficult shot. It was crazy."

Smith, who scored the only Kansas goal, said the same.

"The Nebraska girl hit an unbelievable shot," she said.

Miller added, "If you gave her $100, she couldn't do it again. All I can say is it sucks."

The Huskers took exception because they knew that Baker was capable of doing it again. Didn't matter. She did it this time, and it was remarkable. Some of those on hand even suggested that there was only one other person they could think of who could have scored with their left foot like that.

A 2-1 overtime victory had the Huskers celebrating and Kansas goalkeeper Meghan Miller on the ground in disbelief. (Lawrence Journal-World Photo)

Players and coaches laughed and cried in each other's arms. It was not a national championship, but it felt like that and then some because of all they had been through.

"No one's faced the battles we've faced the last six months," Walker said. "No one has the scars we have"

Finally, this group had something to celebrate, a moment to savor. The Husker felt a debt to Jenna, and they came through. The odds were long, but with no excuses, they pulled off the most amazing victory in the program's 11-year history.

"We weren't supposed to win this game," Miller said.

No, the Huskers were supposed to win that game, and they did, broken hearts and all.

CHAPTER 10

A Tragic Case

⤻

AFTER THE VICTORY OVER KANSAS, the Huskers traveled to Champaign for a Sweet 16 match with Illinois. A controversial penalty-kick call gave the Illini the victory, ending Nebraska's season. Walker and his players were frustrated. It did not seem fair, but that is how the season ended, with the team going farther than anyone could have imagined under the circumstances.

Part of the pain of that last soccer game of the season was the realization that the team would be going home and back to a murder trial and the awful memories of late April. The trial of Lucky Iromuanya had been delayed to allow the team to finish the season.

Few would argue that Jenna's death was the only tragedy in this story. Iromuanya, who had his adult life ahead of him, too, faced charges of second-degree murder, attempted second-degree murder and two felony weapons charges. The proceedings began Dec. 6, 2004, in Lancaster County District Court, with Judge John Colborn presiding. Jeff Mathers and Stephen Schmidt represented the state, the plaintiff, and Korey Reiman and John Stevens Berry represented the defendant. It was a nine-day trial that included testimony from 29 witnesses, mostly people who attended the party at the residence shared by Jenna Cooper and Lindsey Ingram.

Iromuanya had previously claimed he did not intend to kill Jenkins, that his intent was to fire a "warning shot," but the defendant did not take the witness stand during the trial.

Ellen Cooper's emotional testimony, on the first day of the trial, became a source of controversy. Under examination by Mathers, Ellen answered questions about Jenna and the weekend of the shooting.

Asked about her daughter's interests, Ellen said: "She played about every sport you can think of. She skied. She loved horseback riding. She played tennis, ran track. She, you know, loved field hockey, golf. She was an incredible student and she was just involved in a lot of school activities, and she was just an incredibly, incredibly well-rounded person.

"She loved, loved NASCAR. She really got that side of her interest from her father, who loves car racing and her brother, who also does. And she loved motorcycle racing, which her brother was very skilled at."

Mathers later asked Ellen about Jenna's shot-glass collection, which became central to the altercation that led to Jenna's death.

"It was just a hobby with her. I had a sister that collected Derby glasses. They're a glass they make every year for the Kentucky Derby. And Jenna just kind of thought that was so neat, her collection, and it wasn't something she could have afforded to go back and buy the past years. And so it was ..."

After being shown a photograph of Jenna on life support in the hospital, Ellen broke down, crying "that's my baby girl, Jenna" in the courtroom. The defense claimed Ellen's testimony and testimony from others about Jenna's character was not only irrelevant but prejudiced the jury against Iromuanya. Those claims did not hold up with Judge Colborn.

On Dec. 20, the jury returned guilty verdicts on all four counts. On Feb. 24, 2005, Iromuanya was sentenced to life in prison for Cooper's death and to a consecutive term of 25 to 35 years in prison for shooting Nolan Jenkins. Judge Colborn imposed two sentences of 10 to 20 years on the weapons charges.

Before announcing the sentences, Colborn made the following remarks:

"This is a tragic case. It's a tragedy for the family and friends of Jenna Cooper, and for Nolan Jenkins, his family and his friends. And as in any murder case, whenever someone is murdered, there is a sense of loss for

parents, brothers, relatives and friends, and that loss is immense. And when someone is shot and seriously injured, it has a significant emotional impact on the victim, their family, their friends, I recognize that.

"I also recognize that this is a tragedy for Mr. Iromuanya's family and his friends. And I certainly consider the defendant's lack of any real significant criminal history. However, in determining the appropriate sentence, this Court must consider all of the surrounding facts and circumstances of these crimes.

"The jury determined that you intentionally tried to kill Nolan Jenkins, and the jury found you guilty of the murder of Jenna Cooper. You brought a gun with you. No one there had a gun that evening. No one had any type of a weapon that evening, except for you. It was your anger that caused you to pull that gun out of your pocket and you shot that gun in anger. In determining the appropriate sentence, this Court must consider the protection of the public, and I cannot ignore that you shot someone, simply because they pushed you and made you angry. I also must impose a sentence that will not depreciate the seriousness of these crimes."

At the sentencing, Iromuanya was given the opportunity to address the court and the Cooper and Jenkins families. This is what he said:

"First of all, I want to say I'm sorry to Ellen Cooper and her family, and the friends of Jenna Cooper. And I want to say I'm sorry to Nolan Jenkins and his family and friends. In my heart, I know I didn't intend to try to kill Nolan Jenkins. I mean I just know in my heart I didn't, but at the same time, he did get hurt and Jenna Cooper is not here because of me. So I take full responsibility for that and I do believe I should be punished.

"I just... the hardest thing for me is I've got to live with knowing that I'm the reason why she's not here, and that I'm the reason why Nolan Jenkins had to go through what he went through in the hospital. And I just want to say I'm real sorry and stuff for all the pain that I caused to Ellen Cooper and her family, and to Nolan Jenkins and his family. I'm very sorry. That's all."

The Coopers said later they did not believe the apology was sincere. It was forced – "half-ass" is how Billy described it. But Ellen and Iromuanya's mom, Helen, did visit briefly after the sentencing. It was at Ellen's request. She knew that she was not the only mom experiencing great heartache. They hugged as a gesture of that shared anguish.

"I told her I understand her pain," Ellen said. "I felt bad for her pain."

Some of the media coverage of the shooting and trial.

In August of 2006, the Nebraska Supreme Court upheld Iromuanya's conviction but modified the sentence. The change made it possible for Iromuanya to be eligible for parole in 45 years (2051). The original sentence by Lancaster County District Judge John Colborn was for a minimum term of life in prison.

From the Lincoln Journal Star report on Aug. 12, 2006:

The Supreme Court said Iromuanya's sentence in Cooper's death was too harsh, considering Iromuanya's lack of a significant criminal history.

Supreme Court Judge Kenneth Stephan, writing for the court, said: "The court could not have imposed a more severe minimum term for second-degree murder on a hardened criminal with a lengthy history of violent felony convictions. A sentence should fit the offender and not merely the crime."

Under the sentence imposed by Colborn, Iromuanya would have needed to get his life sentence commuted to a set number of years by the state Pardons Board before the state Parole Board could even consider his case.

Now, Iromuanya needs to serve half the minimum sentences on each of the four counts to become parole eligible. Under the decision Friday, Iromuanya is to serve the sentences for the shooting of Cooper and Jenkins at the same time.

William Cooper said he was disappointed by the court's decision to modify the life sentences.

"It troubles me," Cooper said. "I'm not bitter, but I want to keep him behind bars. ... It's my daughter we're talking about."

Iromuanya, in an interview with the Journal Star in April of 2005, said:

"I can understand the anger, even from the judge. I can understand a lot of the anger, so I don't really blame too many people more than I blame myself, because I feel like I'm smarter than that. Even though it happened so quick, I feel like I'm smarter than that.

"It does hurt, because I know one time is enough for me to learn. But Jenna Cooper didn't get another chance, too, so all I can keep doing is praying."

In December of 2011, the Nebraska Supreme Court denied Iromuanya's attempt to be heard over claims he received poor counsel.

The Lincoln Journal Star reported:

The Nebraska Supreme Court again has rejected the claims of Lucky Iromuanya, convicted in the 2004 shooting death of University of Nebraska-Lincoln soccer player Jenna Cooper.

Iromuanya, now 30, is serving 70 years to life for second-degree murder in the case.

He admitted to police he fired the shot that grazed Nolan Jenkins, then hit Cooper in the neck at a party on April 25, 2004, but he said he didn't intend to kill anyone.

At trial, prosecutors argued that Iromuanya did intend to kill Jenkins, and the jury found him guilty.

The state's high court previously had affirmed his conviction on direct appeal, but it reduced his straight life sentence, saying it was too harsh considering his lack of a significant criminal history.

This time around, Iromuanya appealed after he was denied an evidentiary hearing at which he intended to raise allegations that his attorney (Reiman) was inexperienced and ineffective and that prosecutorial misconduct prevented him from getting a fair trial the first time around.

Iromuanya said he would have pleaded to a lesser offense if he had been advised better of the prosecution's plea offers.

At oral arguments in February 2010, his new attorney, Robert Kortus of the Nebraska Commission on Public Advocacy, argued that jurors should have been given instructions that could have led to a lesser manslaughter conviction in Cooper's death.

In briefs to the court, he alleged the trial attorney failed to advise Iromuanya adequately on plea negotiations, whether to testify at trial (he didn't), and to seek a self-defense instruction, among other things.

Kortus also accused the prosecutor of misconduct for appealing to jurors' sympathies in opening remarks and in questioning that elicited irrelevant and emotional testimony from Jenkins.

But in Friday's order, the state's high court said, as it had previously, that whether Iromuanya fired the shot with the intent to kill Jenkins was the critical issue in the case.

And the state's evidence on intent was strong, Nebraska Supreme Court Justice William Connolly wrote.

Because jurors concluded that Iromuanya intended to kill Jenkins, the intent transferred to his killing of Cooper, the court found.

"So while the prosecutor's appeal to jurors' sympathies was improper, the prejudicial effect was tempered by the strength of the evidence and the court's instructions," Connolly said.

And, the high court said, there was no evidence to support a self-defense instruction.

Iromuanya, who was born on May 18, 1981, is serving his sentence at the Lincoln Correctional Center. He is likely to spend the rest of his life in prison, but that is not an absolute since he will be up for parole in 2051.

The fact that Jenna, who often talked about how lucky she was, was killed by a man with that name is hard to comprehend. So is how she died.

And so are the miracles of Jenna, and there are many.

In late May of 2004, this letter arrived on Northfield Drive in Louisville:

Dear Ellen:

On behalf of Nebraska Organ Recovery System and the many patients in need of transplantation, please allow me to express our sincere condolences to you and your family related to the recent death of your daughter, Jenna. Also, I want to relay our heartfelt thanks for your kind and compassionate decision in favor of organ and tissue donation.

I followed the coverage of Jenna's career. She was an amazing young lady and I hope the public outpouring of condolences will be somewhat comforting to you.

I would like to take this opportunity to provide you with some information about the recipients.

The heart was recovered and transplanted into a 39-year-old married lady. We are told that she is doing well and has been discharged from the ICU.

Both kidneys and the pancreas were successfully recovered. One kidney was transplanted into a person was a perfect match for Jenna. The other kidney and pancreas were transplanted into a single recipient. We are told that both of these recipients are recovering well.

The liver was also successfully recovered and transplanted. This person was quite ill prior to receiving this transplant. We are told that this person is also doing well.

Again, let me say how sorry we are about the death of your daughter. We can only imagine the loss and grief you are feeling and we are hopeful that the donation will provide some comfort for you as time passes. Jenna truly leaves a living legacy.

And in October, in the heart of soccer season, Ellen received a handwritten note that said:

Dear Donor Family,

We want you to know that because of your families caring and compassion, my wife Wendy has been reunited with her 1-year-old daughter and her 4-year-old son, after 4 months in the hospital.

Wendy received her heart transplant from your loved one on April 26, 2004. She has experienced a number of life threatening complications but her heart continues to pull her through.

We want to say thank you and may God Bless you and your family.
Sincerely,
Garth and Wendy

Notes from the Author

So what exactly are Notes from the Author?

In this case, they are my white flag waving at perfectionism. These notes are bits and pieces and updates related to Jenna's story – many of them more personal. They are things I wanted to share but just wasn't sure how or where to include them. Like the drawer or box that has some of your special things but with no real sense of organization.

I realize it is unusual to get to this section of a book so quickly, but here we are. I simply decided that the time and stress involved with deciding on the proper placement of these short stories was sinking any chance I had of actually finishing the book. I also had the thought that Jenna's story was not really being shared with many folks while sitting scattered in 46 Word files on my laptop.

And if Jenna and I had anything in common – certainly not soccer skills or speed or looks – it's a struggle with focus and concentration. I can barely finish reading a book, let alone write one.

And that leads me to this.

An apology.

To Jenna's family and many friends and admirers, I am sorry. I am sorry it has taken me so long to finish this project. This book, and Jenna's story, were very important to me, obviously, so much so that I wrestled often with the idea that it had to be perfect, every bit of it. But then I read over and over again these words from Anne Lamott in "Bird by Bird."

Perfectionism is the voice of the oppressor, the enemy of the people. It will keep you cramped and insane your whole life.

I am no Anne Lamott. She is a brilliant, funny (and did I mention brilliant?) writer. We are not in the same league. She's a Hall of Famer. I'm still stuck in the minors. But we are both writers. Her writing just happens to be a lot better than mine.

For example:

> *I think perfectionism is based on the obsessive belief that if you run carefully enough, hitting each stepping-stone just right, you won't have to die. The truth is that you will die anyway and that a lot of people who aren't even looking at their feet are going to do a whole lot better than you, and have a lot more fun while they're doing it.*

Just finish, as they say in soccer. Finish. Writing aside, that is also the way Jenna Cooper lived her life for 21 years, without looking at her amazing feet and those stepping-stones. She continues to teach me and many others about the fun that can come from not looking down and realizing that one of these moments, maybe when you least expect it, is going to be your last. I appreciate that now more than ever.

Easy for me. Much, much harder for Jenna's family and friends, who continue to grieve and always will. If you add it all up, I probably spent a total of 45 minutes talking to Jenna during her time at Nebraska. I do not pretend to have known her like a loved one or close friend. Almost everything I know about Jenna I learned after her death.

But I've learned a lot since then. Enough to fill a 100-page book anyway. In case you were wondering why I decided to write this book more than a decade ago, it started with something Ellen Cooper said the night the Huskers retired Jenna's No. 3 jersey in August of 2004.

"To any parent that's lost a child," she said, "they'll tell you that's your greatest fear, that your child will be forgotten."

That's why this story is so important, and why I had to finish this book, even though it took me way too long to share the story of this miracle worker. We need to remember Jenna Cooper, and we need to see the good in all of the bad. She would.

Every time I would ask a Jenna question of family or friends, I would just hope that I was not adding to the heartache. I have tried to honor the Coopers' requests in every way possible. The title "Heart Felt" was a suggestion from Ellen years ago. I just said, "OK. That's the title. Perfect." The cover photo of Jenna in action – taken by Husker photo ace Scott Bruhn – was also selected by her family.

There are sections of the book that are extremely difficult for Jenna's family and friends to relive. I know that, which is why I made sure the Coopers saw the raw material before it went to print. Again, there are emotions there that I cannot grasp – and that applies to the Davies family as well.

As I was finishing this book in the summer of 2016, the Husker athletic program lost another young star way too soon. Nebraska punter Sam Foltz died in a car accident on July 23. He was 22. My heart goes out to Gerald and Jill and the entire Foltz family. Sam, like Jenna, was a remarkable young person doing a lot of good in this world.

These are tragedies marked by a big "Why?" But the least we can do is try to give God a chance to explain. In the case of Jenna, the miraculous "Why" lives in Green Bay, Wis., with her husband and two children, now both teenagers who still have their mom. Wendy Davies is still here, thanks to Jenna.

There really are no words to explain the incredible range of emotions the Cooper and Davies families were feeling on April 26, 2004. So much grief on one side. So much joy and hope on the other. To lose a child so suddenly at 21. To receive the gift of a heart. How do you find words to do justice to all of it?

My own wide-ranging emotions at the time are still a mystery to me. As I said, I knew Jenna from covering the soccer team, but that was all. She was not a close friend. She was not a family member.

One of my most powerful memories from that time was the big-time cry I had in the office of Nebraska assistant coach Megan Skinner the day after Jenna died. After the news conference held by the soccer team and the athletic department, I stopped in to visit with Skinner for a few minutes, mainly just to see how she was doing. I knew that she and Jenna were close.

Megan had a brave face. She did a good job of hiding her emotions, but I knew she was devastated. She was sitting at her desk. I was sitting across from her. And all of a sudden, I just lost it. There is no other way to describe it.

With all the sadness that was happening around me, it just hit me like a ton of bricks, and out came a ton of tears.

It was all just overwhelming, the tragedy of it. I just wept, with a landslide of emotion. I barely knew Jenna, but it was just all so sad and horrible. It was really powerful and remains a mystery.

I know Megan had to wonder what in the world was happening. I was a journalist and a friend, but on that day I was supposed to mostly be a journalist. And there I was bawling and not completely knowing why. How could Jenna's loss have that effect on me? Whatever forces were going to work in my heart at that time, it's something I will never forget and another reason I felt a calling to share Jenna's story.

When I left Megan's office, I remember Nebraska athletic director Steve Pederson showing people the team's summer camp sign-up sheet. Jenna had put her name down to help with several sessions. That was what she did. She helped. She inspired. And she loved kids. And they really loved her.

John Walker told me how Jenna would look after his daughter, Ally, on road trips. No matter what, for team meals, Jenna would say 'Ally, let's go. You're eating with us.'

That was Jenna.

Many of the Jenna stories in the book come from Walker. He has given a lot of his time to make sure she is not forgotten. It was John who said in August of 2004, "Every player who comes to Nebraska will know the story of Jenna Cooper." He has done his part.

I have to share the fact that John and I were not always the best of friends. There were times when we would butt heads over the amount of coverage the team received in the Lincoln Journal Star. He wanted more, which I understand. Most coaches do. I wanted to make sure we were giving the majority of our readers what they wanted, from all corners of the sports scene. And in Lincoln, that often meant a lot of Husker football and a little of everything else.

In Walker's defense, he was not the only Husker coach who complained about a lack of coverage, although I never heard it from the football coaches. Not a one. They would have been fine with less, I am pretty sure.

I actually loved covering the Husker soccer team and wanted to justify more coverage because they were always such a fun, exciting bunch, a winning bunch. Walker and I managed our differences over the years, until Jenna died. That put a stop to any difficulties we might have had and strengthened my admiration for the coach.

I view Walker's handling of Jenna's death and his coaching that following season as nothing short of heroic. He seemed to have all the right words – the right mix of serious and humorous. Even at Jenna's memorial service, he joked about how Jenna just wanted to be part of a 'kick-ass' team, and he had everyone yelling and 'raising the roof' for the captain.

She was simply a beautiful person – a true gift from God. Now she is in heaven – shooting 60 mph shots on some poor unsuspecting goalkeeper who has no idea of the power in that left leg, racing her red Jeep, making everyone there feel better. Can you imagine having the charisma to make heaven a better place? I have no doubt this has happened already.

Several years later, I asked Walker if he could sum up his memories of Jenna in a few sentences – a nearly impossible task. He obliged with this:

I think the inspiration in Jenna is that she attacked everything in life with 100 percent effort and enthusiasm. I have two images in my head when I think of her. On the field, I have this image of a flying, risk-taking player, and she always seemed to be moving at top speed.

Off the field, I have this image of her standing in my office door, asking me if I had a few minutes to discuss leadership issues as she attempted to become the best team captain that she could be. The inspiration to me is not in her talent (which was high) but in her effort and willingness to make the players/people around her better.

She brought the most out of others, like on that November day in Lawrence in 2004, when the Huskers pulled off a 2-1 overtime miracle against Kansas. I'm a University of Kansas graduate, but I was not cheering for the Jayhawks that day. I do not know how the Huskers won that game. That victory by Nebraska was one of the most incredible things I have ever seen, in sports, or in life for that matter. Jenna was there. I will always believe that because there is no other explanation.

"I think we did so well that year because we all played with so much heart," Lindsey Ingram said many years later. "We played unselfishly. We played for Jenna. She truly was our captain in the end. She was there and she still is."

So much heart.

Very sadly, history repeated for Walker and the Husker soccer program in May of 2015, when assistant coach Peter Underwood was killed in a car accident near Atlantic, Iowa. Underwood had been with the program for four seasons. The cast of Huskers had changed since Jenna's death, but I can't imagine having to go through that kind of pain with your team twice.

I should note that Walker is one of the most successful coaches in NCAA Division I history with a record of 309-145-33 in 23 seasons at Nebraska. He is one of only 18 coaches in Division I history to have reached the 300-victory milestone.

The Husker soccer program has a rich history, started by Walker in 1994. Nebraska was the first Big Eight school to add women's soccer as a varsity sport, and continues 23 years later after detours that put NU in the Big 12 and now the Big Ten. The program has eight NCAA Sweet 16 appearances under Walker along with several conference titles, the most recent being a Big Ten championship in 2013.

When I covered the team, from 1999 to 2008, I loved hearing John's cries of "Well done!" to his players when they would succeed on the field. I heard it a lot. They succeeded a lot, with great fight and energy. Attack. Attack. Attack. That is the Husker way, and it's why Jenna wanted to play at Nebraska. It's also why I loved covering the team. They were electric to watch.

And I will never forget what happened at the end of the 2004 season. For some reason, Walker asked me to attend the team's postseason banquet. I thought it was strange, but I was not going to turn down the invitation. Near the end of the evening, Walker asked me to come up to the front of the room. Really strange again.

Waiting for me was a Husker jersey with my name and the No. 1 on the back. I did not think it was something I deserved, but the sentiment was appreciated more than Walker and the team could ever know.

Jenna was right when she said that group had guts. Guts and heart and one heck of a head coach.

"There's nothing in your background to prepare you for this at all," Walker said.

He was prepared. And to John, I say, "Well done."

There is no argument here that the story of Lucky Iromuanya is also tragic. A few journalist friends have suggested to me that his story is also one worth telling. I agree. It just won't be told here, and that is out of respect for the Cooper family. If that seems like poor and partial reporting on my part, I will go ahead and take the heat on that one.

Iromuanya, who turned 35 in May of 2016, is in the Lincoln Correctional Center serving a total sentence of 70 years to life. He is eligible for parole in October of 2051. His next parole board review will be in 2025.

While the Nebraska Supreme Court did reduce his sentence from what was originally a life term, his recent appeals have been denied, including claims that he received bad counsel during the trial. The most recent petition for an early release was rejected by a federal judge in March of 2016.

As you might imagine, the Coopers still have a lot of anger about Iromuanya and the fact he was carrying a gun in the first place. They are glad he is in prison. "It's where he belongs," Ellen once told me. "There were people who knew this guy carried a gun. They should have done something. Does that sound logical to you? Who thinks it's justified to shoot someone?"

But I also know the Coopers feel compassion for the Iromuanya family. After the trial, Ellen asked to speak with Helen Iromuanya. They hugged. Lucky's mom was barely able to speak.

"I think we both knew the pain that we shared," Ellen told me several years after the shooting. "I did say words to her, and she may have said words to me. But it didn't matter. What mattered was hugging each other and sharing the pain that only these two mothers could understand. I didn't wish this pain on anyone. She didn't wish this pain on anyone.

"We both were hopeless in how to get our children back, our happiness back."

Somewhat lost in all of it was the fact another person was injured and could have been killed that night. The first person to get hit with that bullet was Nolan Jenkins. The shot was fired at him. He still has scars of all kinds.

During the trial, Jenkins said he had no intention of starting a fight, but he was upset when he saw Iromuanya having a heated discussion with Jenna. When he found out that someone else had taken the shot glasses, Jenkins said he went to apologize to Iromuanya.

"When I got to him, he pushed me away," he testified. "I was just standing there when I heard this deafening noise and everything went into slow motion. I reached up and grabbed my head and it's warm, and I have blood running down my head, and I look back and Jenna's lying on the sidewalk."

Jenkins lost enough of his memory that he did not recall seeing Jenna in her hospital room. The morning after she died, he asked Ingram how she was doing, not realizing that Jenna was gone. He cried when he told that story in the courtroom.

Jenkins and Ingram were married in the summer of 2005, but it did not last long. Both admitted that Jenna's death, and the emotions they will carry forever from that April night in 2004, had a lot to do with their divorce in 2007.

Like Ingram, Jenkins is also a nurse. He shared some of his thoughts in an email to me in 2012:

I've been an RN for seven years and have an amazing 2-year-old daughter who I spend every minute of my time with when I'm not working.

From the subarachnoid hemorrhage I suffered from being shot in the head, I still have a scar, and still am amazed that I survived. A centimeter to the right and the bullet would have at the very least taken my eye, probably killed me, and most likely Jenna would have never been shot. Hard to believe but a centimeter makes all the difference. And who knows, but maybe a centimeter to the left and nobody gets hurt at all.

It took me months for my brain to recover from the injury. I was doing speech therapy for maybe a month if I remember. I could read words and talk just fine, but things didn't make sense in my head. I compare it to being in a foreign country where you don't speak the native tongue. The only thing I could watch on TV was sports, and I would turn off the sound because I couldn't understand what was being said anyway.

The death of Jenna may have sped up how quick Lindsey and I were married, but had nothing to do with us getting married. I knew within weeks of dating Lindsey that she was someone I wanted to spend the rest of my life with. It didn't work out that way, and there were many factors that led up to us not working out in the long run. We are still friends.

We came up with the idea of naming a boy, if we ever had one, Cooper in memory of Jenna. If I am ever blessed with a boy I still plan on giving him that name. Jenna was a special person with a great personality and would love any of my kids to grow up in any resemblance of her.

Jenna was fun, accepting, creative, adventurous, driven, sweet and a joy to be around. She loved her leather pants, dancing, going to the lake, and of course soccer. She was goal-oriented, competitive and not scared of anything. Jenna was truly a great person, and the sad part is she would have continued to help and positively influence so many people if she was around. We all lost a good one when Jenna was taking from us, but there's a little bit of Jenna in everyone she's met. She knew how to live life.

More recently, when I asked Jenkins for a quick update on his life, he shared that he is living in Phoenix, with that beautiful daughter, now 6. He is in his 11th year as an ICU nurse, and he still thinks about Jenna often.

"She even talks to me in my dreams from time to time."

Lindsey Ingram – now Lindsey McMenimen – has told me about similar dreams. Mostly good ones.

Only recently has Lindsey had bad dreams about Jenna's death.

"I'm not sure why," she said. "Maybe I'm in a place that I can handle that now."

McMenimen is a nurse at UCHealth – University of Colorado Hospital. She lives in Denver with her husband, Kenny, and their young son, Sheamus.

Lindsey said the only thing that kept her going after Jenna's death was soccer and her teammates. She was asked to lead the team in Jenna's absence, and it was difficult.

She has also been kind enough to take a look back at how it all hit her and hurt her, starting with the 2004 season.

Jenna was voted captain for a reason, not me, so I always felt like I was cheating the team. That was tough for me. That entire summer I cried myself to sleep every night, I cried every time I showered and I cried all the time in the car. Those were the times I could hide it from the world. I never wanted anyone to worry about me so I really tried to hide my pain.

I finally made a decision in early September that I had to get over myself and play that last season with every ounce of my heart. I was not perfect, and made mistakes, but I have never pushed myself harder, and that goes for the rest of the team, too. We would meet as a team prior to every game without the coaches. At each of those meetings I made sure to remind everyone that we were going to play this game for Jenna.

I would tell them not to wait to play their hardest, now was the time. The team probably got tired of my Jenna speeches, but I felt that was my job that year, to never let us forget that Jenna would give anything to be playing, so there was no time to be selfish or feel sorry for ourselves. We were the lucky ones and we could not waste this season.

Her marriage to Jenkins lasted a year and a half. Like Nolan, Lindsey shared that Jenna's death was a source of struggle in their relationship.

The whole ordeal – shooting, traumatic brain injury, recovery, murder trial, coping with the loss of Jenna – affected our marriage. We both coped in very different ways, and unfortunately, were too young/immature to really know how to be selfless. We grew apart rather than closer through all of this as a result.

We maintain a friendship and will always be connected. I heard an interesting statistic from a counselor that 80 percent of marriages that experience a traumatic loss (most likely a child, in our case a dear friend at a young age) result in divorce. Really sad. We both know that we were young and did not give the relationship the fight that it deserved. We have both learned from this and are grateful for the friendship we keep today.

Looking back, I really feel like Jenna was put on this earth to teach us all how to be a better sister, daughter, teammate, friend, student and citizen. Everyone you talk to will speak to one of those areas and tell you how wonderful she was at each role. It was her time in life. She had accomplished more as a soul in 21 years than most will in 80 years. She was wise. She is missed so much every day.

*Lindsey (left) and Jenna and some of their Husker
teammates at a team banquet in 2003.*

Brooke Bredenberg is now Brooke Gillotti, and she teaches art at Lincoln North Star High School. Brooke and her husband, Mike, have two little girls – Luci and Zoey.

Mike Gillotti, in the Small Jenna World department, is now the principal at Lincoln Southwest High School. That is where my wife, Anna, works as a secretary, and it's also where all five kiddos in our blended family went to school (with two of them still there and entering the 2016-17 school year as sophomores).

When Brooke and I talked just before I finished the book, I was happy to hear her laughing as she recalled the early morning soccer game that took place after Jenna died, and how she was the one who knew how to access the light switches so the group could use the Husker practice field in those wee hours.

Brooke knew how to turn on the lights because she would be practicing her goalkeeping work at all hours on that field, which is also where she learned how to take those free kicks, like the one she hit against Kansas in the second round of the NCAA Tournament.

"I was like, 'I took so many free kicks in practice, I'm taking this.'"

It was just good to hear the smile in her voice.

Several years ago, Brooke shared with me a funny story about Jenna and a birthday party in Texas. A warning that it's a PG-13 account of what happened that night.

The best memory is my 21st birthday in San Antonio during our junior year and at the Big 12 Tournament. We were playing Missouri and it was my birthday, Nov. 7. My parents were there, and Jenna's mom and brother were there to watch. I played really bad and Jenna still continued to pump me up throughout the game. We ended up losing by 1. I was goalkeeper.

Being goalkeeper that year, with Jenna as my defender, we were pretty close. After the game I just wanted to go back to my room and cry because I was thinking it was my fault we lost and were out of the tournament. She came to my room and said, "You are going out with me and the families whether you like it or not. It is your 21st birthday." So we went out to the River Walk with her mom, Billy, my parents (Randy and Laurie) and also met others there as well.

We all went to a place called Dick's Last Resort, and yes, they are all dicks to you. That is their thing. Throwing napkins, being rude and just having a lot of fun. There was a band and they had Jenna and I go up on stage and be part of their singing, dancing and making music. It was such a blast. We had so much fun hanging out with her family and mine. My dad actually bought me my first drink.

The night is one I will never forget. Jenna is a true friend and true guardian angel. I think about her all the time. I miss her dearly and will never forget what a true friend she was.

Jenna and Brooke

I still marvel at the 15-3 finish of the 2004 Kentucky Derby. There was magic in that finish, with Smarty Jones out in front, and Lion Heart taking second. Christy Harms, a good friend and Husker teammate, was among those who were sure Jenna had something to do with the events at Churchill Downs that day. She wrote:

> *For all of us to feel the significance of that outcome was incredible. We got a call from Ellen in utter disbelief. Ellen knew Jenna was just letting us know she was OK.*
>
> *The sequence of events that led up to the race was something special. Somehow it started raining, we were able to buy $1,000 seats for $10, stand on the edge of the track soaking wet and watch the Derby race fly by right in front of us – absolutely amazing.*

Smarty Jones and Lion Heart were among the favorites, but it is still amazing to me that they finished first and second, and that the 15-3 combination had never finished 1-2 before, and hasn't since.

Thanks to the Coopers, I have been fortunate enough to attend two Kentucky Derby races – in 2009 and 2014.

Both of them were memorable. In 2009, the longest of shots, Mine That Bird, won the race with an incredible comeback. I even had 2 bucks on the winner at 50-1, so that was quite a day. I will not forget it.

And the 2014 race was even more special because my dad was there with me for his first Derby. Again, the Coopers made it all possible. That was the sunny day California Chrome coasted to victory by almost 2 lengths.

The bald guy on the left is the author, and alongside is John Mabry Sr., Rebel and Billy Cooper. A special day at the Derby in 2014, thanks to the Cooper family.

The Cooper family has treated me so well despite the grief that will never go away. They have been so patient, and not once did I feel any pressure from them to finish this book. I have even had the honor of spending two nights in Rebel Cooper's RV, the La Palma. Now that is a set of wheels. I even wrote some of this book in the La Palma, which sits right next to that front yard where Jenna got the soccer bug.

I stayed there by choice, even after the offer of a bed that was actually inside the house. Just felt like "roughing it" out in the Kentucky wilderness. Rebel has become a good friend and a faithful source over the years, my go-to when I have a quick question or a not-so-quick question for the family. He has taken me for rides in Jenna's Jeep. He has shared so much – the good and the bad and the unbearable.

Ellen and Billy have done the same. Just awesome people. And Kentucky truly is a beautiful place. Next on my to-do list is a trip to see Billy race with his ace pit crew (two of them shown here, minus their crew chief grandpa).

Billy's helpers in the garage – Collins, 3, and Kenna, 6. The girls belong to Billy and his wife, Nicole. Kenna was named after Jenna and Nicole's father, Keith Wicker, who died in 2002.

Regardless of what people think of this book, I know that it does not make everything all better for the Cooper family. The book doesn't bring Jenna back. Ellen has shared that the only thing that will ease her pain is when she gets to be with Jenna again. William hurts all the time. I know that. There is a reason the Coopers don't visit Lincoln unless they have to visit Lincoln. It is painful. And Billy has said many times how much he despises April 25.

This was his Facebook post from April 25, 2016:

"I truly hate this day, this is the worst day of my year. I put on a smile and make it through but this day brings back so many terrible memories from that night. Her murder changed so many people's lives and has impacted my world in so many ways. I truly resent sometimes that life must go on without her. This world was a better place with her and while I know she is watching over us every day the pain of her absence is like a knife to the heart. Saying I miss her is not enough to express the void her loss has left in my life. They say time heals all wounds but that's really not true, time helps you understand and accept your new reality. A reality without my sister Jenna Marie Cooper.

I can't thank all of my family and friends who continue to reach out and remember this day even when I want to forget it. Reading all of the texts and messages is so amazing after twelve years and helps me get through the day. Also so many of her teammates and friends message my parents and it means so much!! We went to dinner at her favorite restaurant tonight like we always do as a family and it was so nice to have some smiling faces to enjoy her favorite cherry cobbler with. Love you so much baby sister and miss you like crazy. JMC3♥☐

Special honors, the nice letters, Derby Day, this book – they do not bring Jenna back. They are just pain-killers. They do not last. I know that. Nebraska assistant soccer coach Marty Everding put it so well when he said, "For all of us, the tsunami is at different places." For the Coopers, it crashes into shore every single day.

Jenna was honored by MacDonald Motorsports at Kentucky Speedway before a NASCAR race in the summer of 2004.

The trail to Cooper Cemetery is beautiful but a little too rough for most cars. Jenna's Jeep can get you through the iron gates and to the burial plots. From there, you can walk another 100 yards to a breathtaking waterfall, the place Jenna talked about and wrote about. The scenery is incredible, no matter what time of year.

Jenna is one of 10 family members who are buried there, including her father's parents – Barbara and William Cooper Sr. – and their parents – Eva Lee and Robin Cooper.

Rebel told me years ago that there was quite a story behind his grandfather's death, so I began doing some research (in other words, I began

*Jenna's dad shining up her grave marker. If you continue walking
on that path, past the other family burial sites, you will come
upon a postcard-perfect waterfall. That bench by Jenna's resting
place says HUSKERS in big iron letters across the backrest.*

Googling). He was right. Quite a story, and one his father did not like to talk
about. William Sr. had a lot of hard feelings about what happened until the
day he died. That is why he had his father's remains moved from Nashville to
the family farm. The farther from Nashville the better.

When you search online, there are several different accounts of what happened to Robin and his father, Duncan Cooper. The story that ended with
Robin's murder started with a heated rift between newspaper man and politi-
cian Edward Ward Carmack and Tennessee Governor Malcolm Patterson.

Carmack lost to Patterson in Tennessee's 1908 gubernatorial race, and he
didn't take the defeat very well, using the power of newsprint to rip his rival at

every opportunity. Carmack, as the editor of the Nashville Tennessean, also took vicious shots at Duncan Cooper, a close advisor to Patterson.

Carmack was a congressman and senator who opposed big business. He also made no secret of his views about blacks and whites having equal rights. He was against it, and that was made clear in Tennessean editorials that called for the nation to solve its 'Negro problem.'

Duncan Cooper was known as an honorable Southern gentleman who led a cavalry for the Confederacy and spent time during the Civil War in a northern prisoner of war camp. His business interests included silver mines and newspapers. He gave Carmack his first newspaper job – as an editorial writer for the Nashville American.

Robin Cooper had a reputation as a hard-nosed lawyer with a strong sense of right and wrong. It was Robin who tried to bring some sense of peace to what he knew was shaping up to be a dangerous feud between his father and Carmack.

His efforts were not successful, as you can read in this account from Greg Tucker of the Rutherford County Historical Society:

Duncan Cooper was incensed by the way Carmack was treating his name and reputation in newspaper editorials and let his anger be known. On Nov. 9, 1908, Cooper and his son Robin were walking in front of the State Capitol when they saw Carmack heading for the same corner. Cooper decided to confront Carmack.

Fearing Cooper's anger, Carmack drew a revolver and fired, hitting Robin. The young Cooper was also armed. Although wounded, he drew and fired three rounds. Shot in the head and heart, Carmack was dead before he hit the ground.

The shooting created a political and legal uproar. Robin Cooper was eventually tried for murder and acquitted on a finding of self-defense. Over the next decade, Robin Cooper practiced law in Nashville and served as counsel for several questionable corporate stock offerings. On Aug. 29, 1919, the body of Robin Cooper was found in Richland Creek in west Nashville.

> *At the time of Cooper's murder, Ned Carmack was a 20-year-old law student. He was initially a suspect in the murder, but the police investigation and "reliable evidence" established that he had nothing to do with the murder. Nevertheless, Ned Carmack repeatedly claimed that he killed Robin Cooper to avenge his father's death. He even claimed later to have killed Duncan Cooper by sneaking into his bedroom and suffocating him with a pillow. (The elder Cooper actually died peacefully at his home with family at his bedside.)*
>
> *No one believed Ned's claims, and no one was ever tried and convicted for the Cooper murder.*

And that is why William Cooper Sr. was so bitter about his father's death and what he viewed as an unacceptable effort on the part of authorities to find out who was responsible. Edward Carmack is despised in many circles to this day, and there is actually a movement to have his statue removed from the State Capitol plaza in Nashville.

Quite a story, as I said, and I believe there is some parallel to Jenna's story. Like her great-grandfather, Jenna was trying to help bring peace to a bad situation, shots were fired, and it did not end well.

Jenna's dad told me that his grandmother, Eva Lee, moved her family to France after Robin's death to make sure they were safe.

"(My dad) had always been very angry about the fact there was no real investigation concerning my grandfather's murder," Rebel said. "The Carmack family made sure of that. A lot of politics involved. My grandmother didn't feel she could protect her three kids or herself, so she packed up and moved to France to live with her sister."

They were there for three or four years.

"I do know that Dad could speak French as well as he could English at that time."

I find it all fascinating, but again, this is not fun conversation for a family that has had to deal with two murders in a century's time. That is incredible to me, and I have to believe Jenna now knows what happened to her great-grandfather.

You can find a lot more on this by doing an Internet search using "Carmack Cooper" as the key words.

The geese. What about all the geese? I have always been sort of mesmerized by this part of the story over the years, mainly because of what happened at the Abbott Sports Complex when they retired Jenna's No. 3 jersey in August of 2004.

The evening they retired her No. 3 jersey at Abbott Sports Complex, it was a lot like the day I met her, warm and sunny, and the geese came so close to us, you could reach up and grab one. I remember standing next to Liz Merrill, a friend and fellow reporter from the Omaha World- Herald, and the two of us saying "Did you see that?" It was remarkable, with 11 or so geese – I have a vision of 11 in my head – flying in just a few feet overhead. There are always geese. I see them and I think of Jenna and her story all the time.

I remember sharing the story of Jenna's heart with my son, Jack, when he was about 6 or 7. Out of the blue, he asked me a question about Wendy, and the exchange went like this:

"Since she has Jenna's heart, does she love the same things or different things?"

"Now that is a good question, Goose."

Yes, I call my son "Goose," and I really don't know why or when or how it started, but it was around the time of Jenna's death. We are going to call it a Jenna thing.

And as I finished this story on a hot, muggy August day in 2016, I was stopped time and time again by the honking of geese flying over our house in South Lincoln. Jenna, surely, saying it's time to finish.

I think it's important to share that Jenna was not perfect. She struggled in school at times, although her grades were always solid. She struggled with confidence. Like all of us, she had her flaws, but when I asked family and friends to talk about her shortcomings, they were usually stumped. She really was an extraordinary young woman.

In a journal Jenna wrote for school as a junior at Sacred Heart, she highlighted a quote: "Each day is God's gift to you. Make it blossom and grow into a thing of beauty."

That was followed by this to-do list for August 24, 2000 (and by the way, she noted that Christmas was just four months away).

What can I do by 12:00 tonight to make the day blossom?

- *Befriend everyone at school, talk, listen, ask questions.*
- *Play my best at practice*
- *Go support the field hockey team*
- *Support the volleyball team*
- *Tell my mom about my day*
- *See my dad*

Wondering if that daily list now includes "Check on Wendy."

Her mom shared with me a story of Jenna's first visit to a new dentist during a trip back home while she was in college. Pardon the dental pun, but she made quite an impression. Ellen said after the appointment the dentist took her aside and basically said, "Wow. Who is that young woman? That is some daughter you have."

Jenna was just really good at impressions – first and last. One of her best friends, Tracy Bender, described her as "beauty, grace, humility, tenacity, guts and glory." All of that and then some. That is why both the University of Nebraska and Sacred Heart Academy have honored her in a number of ways.

Jenna's No. 3 jersey is retired at Nebraska, where the soccer program also named the team meeting room in her honor. Her No. 15 jersey has a special place at Sacred Heart, and each fall, the Valkyries play rival Assumption in the Jenna Cooper Cleat Cup game, around the time of her birthday in late September.

One of her great strengths was her ability to make others feel better about themselves. Many of the letters the Cooper family received after Jenna's death talked about how she often went out of her way to include "outsiders" in her group.

At Sacred Heart, Jenna was known as much for her kind heart as a classmate as she was for her soccer talent. She hated to see any student excluded from a group. You hear about all of the anti-bullying efforts that are just now starting to take hold across the country. Jenna was on the case long ago.

Befriend everyone.

A great tribute. Jenna's No. 15 jersey has long since been retired by the school, but her spirit has had some kind of staying power. I was fortunate enough to attend the 2016 Cleat Cup in Louisville – at Sacred Heart – and there were No. 15 shirts everywhere, on both sides. The place was packed. My favorite memory of that night was seeing every player lining up to hug the Coopers after the game. One by one, they took turns paying their respects.

This photo from the 2013 Cleat Cup game says it all:

It is worth noting that the girls in this photo are not from Sacred Heart. They are from the rival school, Assumption, which is where Jenna's mom went to school. Overwhelming respect for Jenna's memory and legacy on display.

The Cooper family received hundreds of letters and e-mails of support after Jenna died. I have a folder filled with copies of notes about what a great role model she was, what a great friend she was, what a great person she was, with very few mentions of her soccer talent.

When I go through them, I am just blown away by the outpouring of love for this person and her caring spirit. One of my favorites was typed up neatly by a young girl from Beatrice, Neb., and it came with a special gift for the Coopers. No edits here (other than to remove a last name). This is just at is appeared when the Coopers received it.

> *Dear Mr. and Mrs. Cooper,*
>
> *Hi. My name is Madelyne. I was a huge fan of Jenna's. She was the person that I wanted to be. I play soccer for the Beatrice Nitro, and I'm almost 12. I started playing soccer when I was in 3rd grade. That's when I found out about Jenna. It was when our whole soccer team went to Nebraska soccer game. The game was against Brigham Young, on Oct. 17, 2001. All of my teammates were looking for a girl on the field that had the same number as them. They all found one but I hadn't. Instead I spotted your daughter. She was awesome and I new from then on she was my role model. After the game I raced to her to get her signature on the front of my program. It must have been the night she got her picture on it. I was so glad I finally got her signature. I still have that program, it has one rip in it and that's because I was holding it so tight. Since the lost of your daughter I wanted to give this program to you, I figured that it would mean a lot more to you than it would ever mean to me. I made up a little poem, it goes like this: Anything that happens in the hands of God happens for a reason, and everything happens in the hands of God.*
>
> *Jenna's #1 fan,*
> *Madelyne*

There were thousands of reasons why Jenna Cooper came to Nebraska. Madelyne is one of them. I love this because it speaks to the "why" question and the good that came from Jenna deciding to share her talents with Nebraskans of all ages.

Madelyne, with this work, joins the legions of writers who put me to shame. As for that program...

I was not in Louisville for Jenna's Kentucky memorial service at the Cathedral of the Assumption, but I saw the photos, powerful photos of the Huskers in uniform in that church.

I never imagined, and certainly never hoped, that I would be part of a similar scene. But unfortunately that happened in December of 2007 when Lauren Johnson died of leukemia at the age of 13. Lauren was a superstar, the heart and soul of the YMCA's Chaotic Llamas softball program, a group I coached for several years.

Lauren had battled cancer again and again. Such a warrior with such a great sense of humor and spirit. Apparently, heaven was in need of a sharp-witted young woman who loved the Huskers and The Beatles.

Lauren's parents, Jon and Jill, asked if the team would sit in the front rows at Westminster Presbyterian in their red Llama jerseys. This was certainly not NCAA Division I soccer, but what are the awful odds that I would find myself in that picture, like John Walker, sitting in the front of a church with a wonderful group of young ladies, in uniform, saying goodbye to a fallen teammate?

Jenna was there. She helped me again. And like Jenna's Husker teammates, our girls were so strong and brave and funny. "We Play For LJ" became our cry. The Llamas yelled it before the service, in the church, for all to hear.

But no matter how badly I felt, it was 1,000 times worse for Lauren's parents and her little brother, Ben. The Johnson family has had more than its share of dragons to slay. Lauren's dad continues to struggle with kidney problems. Past transplants, including one made possible by his amazing wife, Jill, have not quite done the trick. He has a rare disease called IgA nephropathy, and finding a match is difficult, but not impossible.

This story is for Jon, and it's for Boz Tabler, Jenna's uncle who is in need of a liver transplant. The Tablers have been extremely kind to me during this journey, starting with the beautiful fall day when Boz's wife, Sandy, who is Ellen's sister, showed me around the Sacred Heart campus 12 years ago. She showed me where Jenna played soccer and where they keep her framed No. 15 jersey.

"She was beautiful," Sandy said. "She was loving. She cared so much about people and their feelings."

Jenna is working for Boz in search of a liver, I'm sure of it.

This story is for Peter Salter, a friend and wonderful writer and editor who has helped me with this project over the years with great guidance. Peter, the first person to tell me that Jenna had been shot that Sunday morning 12 years ago, has had major heart problems in his 40's. Like Wendy, he is too young to have major heart problems. He might very well need a new one someday.

This story is for Peter and Jon and Boz and Jenna's dad, who was battling some serious heart problems of his own as this book was being completed. It is for the 120,000 people in our country who are waiting for healthy organs to help them survive. Sign up to be a donor. It's as simple as a visit to www.organdonor.gov.

While in high school, Jenna wanted to be a doctor, or at least she thought she wanted to be a doctor. Having so many of them in the family had a lot to do with that. And she joked about how her surgical approach to organizing food on her plate was preparing her for that line of work.

She wrote in a school project at Sacred Heart: "I can say one day after saving a life that I owe it all to the way I prepare my food."

There was a snag, though. She found out she didn't quite have the stomach for it. Jenna realized that after watching her dad get a broken ankle repaired after a racing accident. So that was the end of that career path, and she eventually decided that mechanical engineering was more her calling.

Three of Jenna's uncles are doctors, and all three were on hand for a gathering at a Louisville restaurant on April 25, 2006. Family members and friends agreed that they would always get together on the anniversary of Jenna's death to celebrate her life at one of her favorite places – Austin's. In 2006, the celebration was originally scheduled for April 23, but because of bad weather, it was postponed for two nights.

The group of about 30 was enjoying dinner in a private room when a server rushed in to ask if there were any doctors available to assist a choking victim. Because of Jenna, there were three doctors and a nurse on hand. Witnesses said the woman would not have survived without the attention of those medical professionals.

Another miracle of Jenna, and there are many. I believe in them. I really do.

This one is certainly not the life-saving variety, but I recall one little miracle on a February day in Lincoln three years after Jenna's death. I was in the parking lot of a Walgreen's when I noticed a stalled car in the intersection just outside the store. The woman who was driving did not know what to do. I offered to help, although I really had no idea what I was doing either.

I fiddled around under the hood for a few minutes, helped wave traffic around the vehicle, and basically played pretend mechanic. I just remember thinking that Jenna would know what to do. She would have had that car moving in no time. Lindsey always talked about how it was Jenna that kept her car running when they were roommates.

I asked the woman to give it a turn. Like magic, the car started. I had done nothing, really, except to have asked Jenna for assistance. A few minutes later, I was driving down 27th Street in South Lincoln. I came to a stop at a light, and there were two cars in front of me – one with one of those "Don't take your organs to heaven…Heaven knows we need them here" bumper stickers; the other with a name on the back windshield – "Jenna."

And in September of 2008, I received an email from a man named Mark Clymer, who is with Ameritas, a large insurance company based in Lincoln. He knew I worked at the Journal Star and wanted to let me know about an experience at Lambeau Field.

I was in Green Bay on Monday night and attended the Packers-Vikings game. I saw a person a couple of rows away from me with a Nebraska hat on, so naturally I went and said 'hello' to him. He told me his wife had Jenna Cooper's heart. He told me you were very familiar with the story – more so than others. I wanted to let you know that they all seem to be fine. He had his son with him, and it was very heartwarming to hear what happened.

It was Garth and Luke Davies, of course, with Husker gear that I had brought to them when I visited Green Bay in 2006. Small Jenna World once again.

That 2006 trip to Wisconsin marked my first and only meeting with the Davies family. We have talked and exchanged messages several times since then, but that is the only time I've been to Green Bay. It was in January of

2006, and it was actually balmy for that time of year – overcast, with temperatures in the 30s.

At that time, Luke was 6 and Emily was 3. They welcomed me into their home in Luxemburg, just outside of Green Bay – a cozy place tucked away in the woods.

Before the trip I received the bad news that Wendy could no longer see. She lost her sight in 2005 because of a terrible infection – aspergillosis. According to the Centers for Disease Control and Prevention:

It is caused by Aspergillus, a common mold (a type of fungus) that lives indoors and outdoors. Most people breathe in Aspergillus spores every day without getting sick. However, people with weakened immune systems or lung diseases are at a higher risk of developing health problems due to Aspergillus. The types of health problems caused by Aspergillus include allergic reactions, lung infections, and infections in other organs.

Yes, one more dragon the Davies family had to slay.

Garth was in sales (and still is). Luke and Emily were into everything. When I visited, Emily, a little blonde, was riding her bike around the kitchen island. Around and around, and in her, I saw Jenna. Wendy couldn't see Emily racing around, but she had no trouble dodging the little speed-wheeler as she worked in the kitchen. You really couldn't tell that she had no vision. I was impressed with her ability to find her way around.

I was also introduced to the Tundra Head. It was Garth's creation, mad Packer fan that he is. It is a heavy Styrofoam square to wear on your head at Lambeau Field to celebrate the famous frozen tundra. Think Cheesehead but with grass.

We talked for over an hour, with SpongeBob on the tube in the background, and the kids, like all kids that age, getting restless. Then we went out for a nice meal at Brett Favre's Steakhouse and had a great visit. I was honored and grateful that they shared most of that Saturday with me.

*This beautiful family is the Davies family, in a portrait
taken about two years after my visit.*

The Davies talk a lot about miracles. And who could blame them?

"(Wendy) was getting to the end. She wasn't doing well at all," Garth said. "We just started praying and crying. We went to bed (April 25), and the next day the heart was there.

"It's just miracle after miracle."

In the end, this story is about Jenna and finding the good in tragedy and not forgetting her. It is about God and faith, and it's about a heart. It is some heart. Jenna got it ready for the next stop. Just ask Wendy. It's been 12 years since she found life again.

There were moments of uncertainty about how long she might survive. Dr. Johnson said it was a rough road, rough still, but like the letter from Garth and Wendy said, "the heart continues to pull her through."

It pulled her through the fight with aspergillosis, and it pulled her through a cancer battle in 2012 – post-transplant lymphoma, blood cancer.

Wendy went through chemo, and Garth said "everything seems to be OK with that."

So much of the battle has not been OK.

"She was sick for so long, just absolutely sick, with the transplant, then the infection that damn near killed her," Garth said. "We would just say, if something would come up that was life-threatening, we just have to slay a frickin' dragon today. We have to slay another dragon."

You don't slay dragons without the right tools. Wendy has been blessed with the equipment she needed to win all of these heavyweight fights.

"This heart has been beautiful for Wendy," Johnson said. "It really has been wonderful."

The Cooper and Davies families have never met in person. They have both talked to me about how they hope to meet someday – "I would love that," Ellen told me – but as of Nov. 1, 2016, that had not happened. And it's certainly not up to me to make it happen or even suggest that it should happen.

I have seen made-for-TV events involving donor and recipient families, and every time, I thought the same thing – those TV cameras should not be there for something so personal and so powerful.

I do know the Davies family is grateful beyond words.

"You don't really know what to say," Garth said. "That's a pretty big thing, you know what I mean?"

"It's quite a miracle."

Those miracles. They sure are cool.

I love the fact that Wendy's birthday is on Valentine's Day. I love the fact that their kids, now 13 and 16, have their mom. I love the fact that Emily is a soccer star.

"She can just boom the ball," Garth said. Dad even thinks she's got a chance to be the first female punter in the NFL someday. I can see Jenna and Sam Foltz conspiring on that one.

For now, the most prominent symbol of the Cooper-Davies bond hangs in a special place in the Davies' home. It's a shirt that William Cooper sent to them from one of the Nebraska-Louisville soccer matches played in Jenna's honor. Garth had it framed and hung over the stairs.

"Every time (the kids) come down the stairs, they see it," he said.

Garth sent me this Smartphone photo of the framed Jenna shirt that hangs in their home for all to see.

A nice gift, but not quite as amazing as the other gift the Davies received from the Coopers.

That's a pretty big thing, you know what I mean?

"This heart that she's got has been an Olympian-type heart," Garth said. "With all the complications she's been through, that heart just keeps going."

Like a waterfall rushing through the woods of Prospect, Kentucky.

That heart keeps going.

Maybe my favorite photo of all. Jenna's nieces, Kenna and Collins,
putting flowers on Jenna's memorial. The marker says, "Sleep
Softly Sweet Jenna. Shine On Bright Star That You Are."

Gratitude

THIS SECTION COULD TAKE ANOTHER 12 YEARS. THERE ARE SO MANY PEO-
PLE who have helped me with this project. Some have shared stories, often
through tears. Some have encouraged. Some have edited. All are appreciated,
more than they could ever know.

I'm not going to make a futile attempt to list everyone here, but for starters, I want to thank the Cooper and Davies families for all of their time, help,
support and courage. They have been through so much, and yet they still
let this stranger into their lives and homes. I am so grateful for all they have
shared. That goes for many members of the Husker soccer family as well.

Through this process, I have learned the importance and value of having
cheerleaders in our lives, the way Jenna was a cheerleader for the people in her
life. It's also important we thank those cheerleaders as often as we can. No one
was rooting harder for me to finish this book than my wife, Anna. I'd be lost
without her, and the same goes for my sister Mimi, who is a saint.

Thanks to writer and journalist friends John Horan, Cindy Lange-
Kubick, Peter Salter, Kelly Madigan, Dr. J. Kemper Campbell, Clark Grell
and Julie Koch for their help and cheerleading along the way. And big thanks
to Scott Young, my boss at the Food Bank of Lincoln, where I have been the
development director since 2011. Scott is a great encourager and my professor
of gratitude.

I am thankful for my amazing children (now amazing adults) and their
mom, Molly. And I am thankful for a mom and dad who would do anything

for me, and pretty much have. Two wonderful cheerleaders. Both have helped me through many difficult times.

It was a thrill to take my dad, John Sr., to his first Kentucky Derby in 2014 (thank you, Cooper family). And my mom, Melissa, gave me a big boost on this project years ago when she sent me a note that included the following verse from 1 Samuel 16:7.

The Lord does not see as man sees, for man looks at the outward appearance, but the Lord looks at the heart.

Like Jenna said, it's about what's underneath the surface. It's about the heart. And the heart is a funny and remarkable thing. Mine has been under some inspection itself.

I had a stroke on Sept. 28, 2016, on Jenna's 34th birthday, if you can believe it. It was also the day before my 51st. It was a real stroke, complete with slurred speech, facial droop, loss of coordination, the works. It happened first thing in the morning while I was getting ready for work, and I was fortunate that Anna and my son, Jack, and stepdaughter, Ashley, were there to make sure I got to the hospital quickly. They saved my butt, no doubt about it. So yes, I have a lot to be thankful for.

Since it happened on Jenna's birthday, I had to wonder if she was trying to put a stop to this book nonsense. She never wanted any fuss. But the way things worked out in my favor so quickly – the doctors said my turnaround was astounding – maybe it was just God (and Jenna) providing a stern reminder that life is short, and each day is a gift (and it's time to finish the darn book).

My doctors said the stroke was caused by a large hole in my heart. Some kind of ironic twist for the author, huh? Hard to believe, but true. The hole was repaired at Bryan Heart on Dec. 12, 2016 (thank you, Dr. Robert Hibbard). I had my heart patched up around lunch time, recovered for a couple of hours in Room 303 (no kidding) and went home the same day. The miracles of modern medicine.

My heart is whole, and not just because of that patch job. Being able to share Jenna's story after all these years is also a big part of that. I owe a lot to her. That I know.

Thanks to her, I am a better person, a more grateful person, a more complete person. Thanks to her, I have seen beautiful new places and now have some wonderful and dear friends in Kentucky. That is no small thing. Thanks to her, I have been to two Kentucky Derbies. Because of Jenna, I listen to Smashing Pumpkins. Because of Jenna, I stop and notice the geese, every time. Also, no small thing.

I wrote about the dreams people have had about her – some good, some bad. Some I would never want to imagine. But I had one, too. Just one. It was in 2005, after I wrote a story for the Journal Star titled "The Miracles of Jenna." In the dream, I was in a room with a large group of people. Jenna appeared. She gave me a hug, said thanks, and then disappeared.

That's all I remember about that dream. I don't even recall if I thanked her in return.

To you, Jenna Marie Cooper, my heart-felt thanks.

Just a girl from Kentucky? I don't think so.

Underneath The Surface

By Jenna Cooper
January 15, 2004

I WILL WEAR A DRESS, and sometimes it will be pink. I spend time doing my hair and make-up, and then I will put on perfume. I will talk cute with a little charm, but do not let these things fool you. I am a tom-boy at heart. The things that cannot be seen on the surface are the things that mean most to me. I play soccer, work in the garage, and drive race cars.

I am just a girl from Kentucky. I grew up with a Mom that was always on the cutting edge of fashion, a Dad that races cars, and a brother (Billy) that races motorcycles. My Mom tried her best to make me into a little princess, but for some reason I was drawn to the action.

Growing up with an older brother caused me to be one of the most competitive people that I know. He used to give me such a hard time, and I had no other choice than to fight back. Billy was the one that made me as tough as I am today, and he was the one that got me involved in playing soccer. My Dad sparked my interest in the garage and in racing. Ever since I was a baby I have always been in the pits of the race track. The roaring engines and smell of gasoline get my adrenaline flowing. I guess I could say that racing is just in my blood. The dresses and the fashion sense came from my Mom. I cannot thank her enough for helping to refine me a little. She balanced me out and helped me to become, what I consider to be, a well-rounded person.

That is a little about where I acquired some of my main hidden passions and how they have molded me into the person I am today. When it came time for college, I found out that I had a lot more to learn about the world that I could not have possibly learned living with my family in the same city I have lived in all my life. I needed to find independence and the true me. I moved away from home to play soccer and attend school at the University of Nebraska.

Out here in Nebraska I found love and an emotional side of me that had never been accessed before. After learning of the love, I then had my next lesson in heart break. From this experience I found out what truly was important to me, my family, soccer, school, goals, dreams, passions, and independence. I have grown more than I thought was ever possible from all this. I have become even more of a determined person. A big part of it carries over into my soccer and academic careers.

I love the soccer career I have developed here and I hope to one day be able to continue it after college either playing professional or for the US Women's National team. I am currently in training with the National team, and I enjoy every minute of it. Initially, academically, I came to college with the full intention of becoming a doctor, but it did not take me long to find out that I am a very squeamish person when it comes to bodies and injuries. That is when I decided to switch into the field of Mechanical Engineering. My dreams are to one day be involved in race car design.

I am a strong person, and that is something that I do not take for granted. I do not like to judge people based on their appearance. I like people to know me for me and for the things I care about. I hope one day I can be an inspiration to someone else to follow your dreams and be who you truly are inside.

An average of 22 people die in the United States each day while waiting for an organ transplant.

To be a donor, visit www.organdonor.gov for information on how to register in your state.

Jenna's story lives on. For updates, please visit www.jennacooper3.com

Made in the USA
Lexington, KY
01 April 2017